About the cover design
KonnaKuttan

I've watched him grow from a tender little being into a strong, muscular presence. His girth and height now are a sight for the Gods. His arms and limbs are spread imperiously across the compound.

Meet my favourite companion, standing like a sentinel just outside my window. Known as a Cassia Fistula to science but KonnaKuttan to me! A powerful tree, Konna (in Malayalam), towering over me as I gaze out of my window.

Draped in beautiful yellow flowers, preparing to welcome Vishu with his offerings. A sight that is at once nostalgic and hopeful. Leading me down by-lanes of memories, fondly wandering through past, happy Vishus.

While at the same time, giving me a glimpse of the joys to come. Silently understanding my thoughts and emotions, listening to my soul without judgment. Providing a home to not just the Chairman, my favourite Greater Coucal bird who nestles amongst the branches, but also humming birds, squirrels and bumble bees.

Chairman and KonnaKuttan are quite a team! When the going gets tough, Chairman alights on KonnaKuttan's bosom and lets out a mournful "Ooop ooop ooop" to relieve the stress and sorrow. And, the true friend that he is, Konna Kuttan listens with understanding and moves his leaves almost imperceptibly as if to say, "all will be well"…just as he does with me too. With Vishu around the corner, KonnaKuttan is awash in a sea of yellow.

Magnificent, royal, abundant!
He, Konna, is Thailand's national tree..
A symbol of Kings, wealth and all things auspicious…
But to me he is the symbol of Lord SriKrishna's divine presence so much so that I can almost hear the notes of that sublime flute issuing forth from within the swathes of yellow silk.

Cover design by Reuben K Antony

*To my revered parents
Malathy M Nair and V
Madhavan Nair "Mali":
embodiments of love,
encouragement and
support…and who never
ever
said no to me…
To Radha, loyalty
personified, who's love
has nourished and
sustained me.*

Contents

Gratitude

To Julie, my Editor, who inspires me every step of the way on this journey…

Preface

These are a collection of stories from my life.

They're not meant to be an autobiographical accounting of my years on this planet.

Neither are they in chronological order.

Rather, they're milestones marking the long road I've taken.

A road that's been full of inclines and declines, potholes and smooth drives, traversing lush valleys and barren deserts.

But a drive, nonetheless, replete with fulfilment and loads of memories, some beautiful, some painful…

Loads of lovely people have crossed my path.

Some have hurt me but many others have lavished happiness on me. And everything's been for the good!

This is not a normative or prescriptive story. Its just my story.

For the better or the worse.

The story of a lifetime!

V.K. Madhav Mohan

2025

1. Kunhikannan

It was a cool morning in January 2005. Kochi was as pleasant as it could get! As I got into my car at 7 am to drive to Subhash Park, I was pretty relaxed and looking forward to meeting and walking with my friends from the Good Life Association (GLA). This was a grouping that I'd created; members were all regulars at the Subhash Park, people with whom I'd spent many wonderful years walking every morning by the backwaters bordering one of the few green lungs of Kochi.

As I parked my car and entered the Park on foot I was beset by a strange sense of foreboding. Something that I just couldn't put my finger on; a kind of disquiet. In the distance I could make out the rather roly-poly figure of Suresh walking briskly ahead of me. Salim was by his side and I could see the usual excited gesticulations as they talked. I sped up and caught up with them.

Both of them turned around and saw me. I could see that both of them looked uncharacteristically glum. Instantly I knew that something was not quite right. The sense of dread was becoming a tragic reality.

"What happened? "I asked. Suresh was the first to answer; clearly, Salim was struggling with emotion.

"Its Kunhikannan. What about him? He died last night.

Are you sure, Suresh?

Yes. He was riding home on his motorbike late last night, speeding to get home quickly. Suddenly from a by-lane a cyclist bolted onto the main road and Kunhikannan had to apply the brakes, especially the front brake. He flew over the handlebars and landed on his head. He wasn't wearing a helmet. Died instantly, on the road where he fell."

I was stunned. Just yesterday morning we had seen him practising Karate under the large Rain Tree while we walked past. He'd made this spot his own. Everyday he'd turn up at 7.30 am, first do warm ups and then practise Katas that Sensei Kuppusamy had taught him in the Shorin Ryu Karate Dojo.

And that was our special connection: Sensei Kuppusamy. I was amongst the first students to enroll in Sensei's class when he first came to Kerala in 1977 and commenced Karate classes at the Cochin Arts Club (CAC) auditorium on the second floor of the building on I S Press Road, just off Banerjee Road.

And now, Kunhikannan was no more. Just like that. Gone in the twinkling of an eye. Unbelievable and so, so very sad.

Kunhikannan was a very affectionate presence in the Park. He'd greet us with a cheery "Good Morning" when we walked past the Rain Tree. Tears were streaming down Salim's cheeks.

For me, it was even more of a painful blow because of our mutual closeness to Sensei. No doubt, Kunhikannan joined the Dojo many years after me but we knew each other well. Every time he saw me, he'd address me as Sempai (the Japanese term used to describe a senior student of the Dojo) and bow with love and respect. All the memories of the Dojo and Sensei and seeing Kunhikannan train with zest flooded my consciousness.

My instinct was to go to his home immediately and do what I could to console a no doubt disconsolate family.

"Does anyone know where he lived?" I asked.

"No. Let's find out. And go as soon as we can."

The three of us asked around. Later that afternoon Salim called me with the exact location and address. We planned to go next morning.

Antonychettan was affectionately nicknamed "Payyans" by the GLA because of his youthful enthusiasm for life despite being a septuagenarian; he too joined us for the condolence visit. It was a long drive. Unending, because of the pall of gloom that hung over us like a black cloud. A sombre silence cloaked the inside of the car. After 2-hour journey traversing narrow village roads, full of twists and turns and bumps and jerks we finally arrived at Kunhikannan's home.

It was a heart-rending sight! A small, decrepit two room cottage. A young wife. Three daughters, the oldest about 5 years old. No source of income. And now the breadwinner and sole source of security for the family… taken away. The lady was in a daze beyond tears and words. We just stood around for a few moments.

And then, she looked at me and her eyes widened in recognition. Slowly and with hesitation she pointed to a an old, framed, faded photograph hung just above the front door beyond a small verandah.

What a shock!

There, in the midst of a long-gone happy time, some thirty years earlier, I stood with Sensei and other students, a faded photograph fresh in memory. She said in a halting, grief-stricken voice,

"Saarine enikku ariyam. Kunhikannan eppozhum parayarundu."

"I know you, Sir Kunhikannan. I used to talk about you and Sensei and all the good times."

Then she said in Malayalam: "I'm totally broken. We have a house loan from the Cooperative Bank. Kunhikannan has not been able to pay the monthly instalments for the last 6 months. The Bank sent a final notice last week. If we don't pay the arrears within a month, they'll auction the house. Now he's gone. We have no way to repay the Bank. We will lose this house."

For once I was speechless.

Imagine a young widow with three baby daughters on the street with no money and no protection. Fair game for every predator of the worst kind!

I decided then and there that we would not let that happen, not when I have breath left in my body.

After a bit, I gathered up my wits, mustered up some semblance of balance, took a leap of faith and said, "Don't worry. We'll see that you don't lose the house."

On the drive back we talked about the direst of straits Kunhikannan's untimely demise had forced his defenceless family into. We discovered that he had consumed alcohol just before embarking on his fateful final motorbike ride home. So, there was no way the insurance company would entertain any claim. That meant that the family was without a shred of cover.

I was clear that a piecemeal approach or ad hoc donations would only be band aids. So, I resolved to find a root cause solution. I decided to solve the house ownership problem once and for all. Suresh talked on phone to the hapless widow and found out the exact bank liability. And then we called a meeting of all the Good Life Association members next morning at the Park.

"Good morning, ladies and gentlemen. Today we have a duty and within it an opportunity to make a life and death change in the life of a family distraught by tragedy. Our dear friend Kunhikannan's family is on the verge of being thrown into the street where they'll be at the mercy of pimps and crooks. To prevent that from happening we have to pay the cooperative bank Rs 75,000/- immediately. I earnestly appeal to each one of you to join me in contributing to save the future of one young woman and three girl children. Whatever you can give, no matter how small, will be invaluable." Right then my good friend Amarjit Singh, God bless him, piped up and said, "Please put in whatever you can and I will donate the balance to make up Rs 75,000/- "

And so, in a matter of minutes we collected nearly Rs 1 lac!! (INR 100,000/-)

The very next day Suresh and Salim drove back to the village. We asked the young widow to come to the bank. The bank manager was astounded. So was she. Here was a set of unrelated people carrying cash to pay up the entire loan outstanding of a deceased borrower!

Not only did we clear the entire dues but we also ensured that the bank released the title deed to the house then and there; only after handing it over to Kunhikannan's widow at the bank did Suresh and Salim leave!

We, the Good Life Association, had made sure that the family was safe and had a home in which they could rebuild their lives.

We had chosen not to contact the family thereafter.

It's now more than 20 years since that day at the bank.

Hearsay is that they're all doing well.

What more can we ask!

2. Crowbar On Flesh

It was a Friday afternoon in 1983. There it was, a dull scrunch. Wait, was it a branch falling off the tree in the yard or some load falling off a handcart? Once, twice, now again, a third time!

I emerged groggily from the depths of reading, thinking and writing my weekly economic analysis, Infodat.

Having quit my job as an officer with State Bank of India, my income had stopped abruptly. There was no more pay check arriving with the certainty of dawn after a month of toil. I was desperate. I had to come up with some idea to earn something, anything!

Necessity being the mother of invention, Infodat was the saviour. It was a 2-page summary of the week's economic and business developments. Crisply written, peppered with puns and analysis, it was designed for time pressured Managing Directors (CEOs were unheard of in the early 1980s); it was meant for people who needed a quick summary of happenings in India's economy.

I sold about 100 annual subscriptions at Rs 600 per annum[1]. That kept me afloat, till I came up with the next idea! There's

---

[1] *Present value of Rs 60,000/- in 1983 is Rs 9,61,360 in 2024, adjusted for an average annual inflation of 7% ; source: ChatGPT*

nothing quite like figuring out where your next rupee is coming from to keep your creative juices flowing!

And so, every Friday, week after week for 52 weeks running and then for 5 years thereafter, my nose was put to the grind. I read up every economic and business newspaper available. Macro and micro developments in the economy were bewildering and tested my understanding to the limit. I would put my spin on them and then churn out a two-page summary which would be typed, corrected, cyclostyled (no photocopies then!) and mailed out every Saturday afternoon. On Monday mornings Infodat would arrive on the desk of the subscriber.

On Fridays I was lost to the world!

So, it was a jolt when I heard that sickening sound, once, twice and now thrice and it jerked me back into my surroundings. It was too gut wrenching to ignore. I peeped out of the window.

A crowd had gathered outside my house. They were abusing someone. One of them had a metal rod, a crowbar! The mob was getting worked up. Clearly, they were dispensing mob justice. The lynch mob that alas, is always lurking in the shadows, waiting to be stoked, was rearing its ugly head…

I rushed into the crowd.

What I saw horrified me. An anger that I didn't know I could feel built up. It gave me a strength I didn't know I had. I now know… that was my inheritance, the Warrior Spirit, stirring to life.

An emaciated old man was cringing on the ground.

His sunken eyes glistened with tears. He'd been beaten with the crowbar.

The skin on his starved frame was broken by the impact of the crowbar. His weak bones were about to be smashed.

Hunger and fear leapt out of him and struck deep within me. I roared with fury.

"What's going on here? This old man is a thief. He stole a loaf of bread from this shop. We're going to teach him a lesson," snarled someone.

The crowbar-wielding lout was about to strike again, probably to kill him. That's when the dam broke.

I shoved the man holding the crowbar and wrested it away from him.

It was now my weapon. Ready to be unleashed on anyone who dared to stand up to me.

"How dare you hit this defenceless man? If anyone tries, I'm going to use this crowbar on him like you used on him. If he's a thief, well then, let's take him to the police station. But you're not going to lay a finger on him. Go away, now, right this moment."

My anger did the trick.

Shame overtook everyone present. The crowd melted away.

I was alone with the old man.

I can still remember the look in his eyes. Relief. Thankfulness.

Gratitude for the reprieve from death by crowbar.

That hot, humid Friday afternoon was spared from witnessing a gory murder.

Right there in the middle of the city in broad daylight. So much for a civilised, fully literate population.

The man got up shakily. I gave him some money for food and sent him on his way.

I learnt that mobs have a mind of their own. I understood then how easily people are manipulated into committing the most heinous crimes.

That's a sobering thought that has remained with me.

Every time I see TV reports of political rallies and hate crimes, the sound of crowbar on flesh flashes before my eyes.

3. Mornings with Amma

The front door was wide open!

There she was, sitting on the sofa facing the entrance.

A sight to behold!

Crisp white saree with a pale blue blouse.

Long hair left open, still dripping after the cold-water bath. A smile more beautiful than a million sunrises.

Imperial.

Stronger than steel. Courage personified. Fearless.

Tender and loving.

Loyally sincere in every breath.

The very definition of encouragement. Divinity in human form.

Embodiment of the purest, most tender, motherly love. Amma.

As I sauntered into her apartment every morning after my walk and workout she'd say, "Here, drink it while its hot", handing me a large steaming mug of the best coffee in the world.

Filled to the brim. Overflowing with love.

Nowhere else can I ever hope to get a better welcome!

The conversation would drift from subject to subject. From local news to who's who and what's what. We would travel around the world. Taking stock of everything that happened in the last 24 hours. Current affairs, culture, music & dance and especially, sports! Nothing was beyond her ken.

She was not only current, but irreplaceably relevant until very the last breath!

Amma created waves by enrolling in our computer classes at the age of 75. Several newspapers gushed over the Grandma hitting a QWERTY keyboard!

She wrote, chanted and learnt everything.

We'd talk about every little thing. She'd give me a quick roundup about what every relative was up to! That's because she was in regular touch with everyone.

Her home was a magnet for everybody. Affection and hospitality were always on tap. So, her social circle and friends were all in contact. Every day someone or the other was visiting!

And there would always be the tastiest food in copious quantities.

She even had a secret recipe for her trademark dish: pazham nurukku. Kerala bananas stewed in jaggery and ghee. Just one little whiff of it could send you to heaven! No cryptographer has ever been able to crack that recipe's code!

After about an hour I'd get up to go back to my home & office. "Amma, I've got to go now."

"Irrikkada, oru cup kaapi kude kudichittu poya mathi…sit down you busybody, you can only leave after drinking one more cup of coffee".

Not that I needed much persuasion!

She'd disappear into the kitchen and soon all kinds of mouthwatering smells would waft into the living room.

The entire home bathed in the fragrance of her presence.

And then Amma would reappear in a jiffy with the crispest of dosas and tons of chutney.

"Amma, I can't eat all this. Shut up and eat. I'll give you the coffee after you finish the dosas."

It all began with one cup of coffee, leading to dosas galore and then coffee again.

Interspersed with conversation, banter and loving care.

Her coffee was only surpassed by her anxiety for me to be happy and recognised.

And that was my typical morning with Amma! How I wish I could re-live those mornings.

I'd give anything to bask in the glow of her warmth again.

4. Amma Summoned

During one of our mornings together Amma said, "Eda[2], enikku onnu Guruvayurilekku pokanam. I want to go to Guruvayur. I'll certainly take you."

And so it was in mid July 2007 that we arrived at the famous, Sri Krishna Temple at Guruvayur.

It was a balmy mid-morning. The temple is always packed with fervent devotees. They come from all over the world. United in their total surrender to Lord Guruvayurappan. Sri Krishna, the presiding deity of not just the temple but indeed, the entire universe.

Since Amma had a little difficulty walking, we drove right up to the Western Nada (Entrance). This by itself was surprising and unusual. We would normally have to park a distance away and walk to the East Nada. We chose to try and drive up to the West Nada since it would be easier for Amma to navigate. For some reason no one stopped us. Amma alighted from the car right next to the West Nada!

It was quite a sight to behold!

This supremely elegant lady, in an immaculate off-white saree and blouse, holding her son's right hand with a mixture of pride

---

[2] *Eda is an affectionate term in Malayalam that elders use to address someone younger*

and love, with her daughter (in law) hovering protectively by her side, slowly making her way into the temple. We entered the temple precincts to find it crowded, as usual. We had to be careful not to cause discomfort for Amma (who was 80 years young at the time).

As we were turning left and on to the granite concourse, an ethereal presence caught my eye.

It was a clean-shaven elderly man in a cream, silk mundu and matching shawl walking briskly towards us as though he was intent on meeting us. He had the most indescribably attractive aura. Celestial. Divine. Impossible to describe.

He caught up with us a couple of steps into the concourse and came close to me. I felt the lightest of touches on my left shoulder.

"What a great thing you're doing now, bringing your mother, so lovingly, to this temple. You're blessed." It was the softest, most mellifluous voice I'd ever heard.

Before I could turn and thank him, he'd disappeared. No sign of him in the crowd. Vanished into thin air!

Who was he? Anyone I knew?

No. A complete stranger. Why did he say that to me? Soon we were in the sanctum sanctorum.

It was really most unbelievable, unforgettable experience!

The milling crowd of devotees was jostling for a glimpse of Guruvayurappan.

Inexplicably, a path was cleared for Amma. Divine intervention!

The ushers spoke reverentially to her.

"Amma, please pray as much as you want. Stay here as long as you want."

The same ushers who'd shoo you away if you tarried more than 2 seconds before the Deity.

She stood alone before the Deity.

The stream of worshippers went around her like a river swirling around a big rock.

The temple staff were ever so considerate.

Amma stood unmoving, palms together, in total devotion.

It was as if she was engaged in a deep personal dialogue with Guruvayurappan. Time stood still. I don't know how long.

"Come, let's go."

Her face glowed. I knew she was completely fulfilled.

We walked slowly, in silence, out of the temple and got into the car. "Did you see that man who came up to me? "

"Which man?" asked Radha.

Amma was very clear, "I didn't see any man coming to you". I was confounded!

Who was he? How did he single me out?

Back home our mornings continued, full of an affectionate togetherness and coffee!

Nothing untoward, no signals. But she knew and so did I.

And, then, on the 20th of August 2007, in the blink of an eye, she was gone. Amma had attained the Lotus Feet, effortlessly, painlessly, blissfully.

The Lord had summoned her to Guruvayur a month earlier for the profoundest reason.

A few days later it dawned on me. Who had accosted me in the temple? I understood.

5. Cable Break!

To me he appeared like some Greek god!

Tall and heavily built. Sharp sky blue uniform. Gleaming brass.

Mirror shined black shoes. And most awe inspiring of all: wings on his left breast.

The unmistakable insignia of a pilot in the Indian Air Force.

Earned after iron discipline and hard work after first passing the Pilot Aptitude Battery Test (PABT).

The PABT itself is not just any ordinary test. It's the ultimate evaluation of an innate talent to fly. Hand eye coordination, motor skills, reaction time and ability to make quick decisions, all are tested to the limit by placing the aspirant in a simulated cockpit with all kinds of other challenges thrown in. The pass percentage is, naturally, miniscule. And it's administered just once in a lifetime.

Squadron Leader Springer strode into the classroom of our NCC Senior Boys (National Cadet Corps) Air Wing HQ with a larger-than-life impact! It was the first time I'd seen him. He was everything I'd ever wanted to be! A fighter pilot in the Indian Air Force. As a 17-year-old, I wasn't only starstruck, I was simply blown away.

"Well, boys, smarten up!

You, Madhav Mohan and you, Kuldeep Singh, you're the lucky cadets!

You're the only two gentlemen to have passed our unit's selection process with over 80% marks and so the two of you will report to the airfield in full uniform at 0600 hrs tomorrow for glider training.

You'd better be sharp on time and your uniform had better be flawless. And obey your instructor totally, without question, repeat, total obedience. Or you'll be pushing up daisies 6 feet under" he thundered.

"Six feet under pushing up daisies", that phrase still resonates within my consciousness! Imagine someone dead and buried, because he didn't follow the instructor, pushing up daisies from below the surface! Talk about evocative imagery!

From that moment on I began to live a dream.

I'd spend hours polishing the brass on my NCC Air Wing uniform till it shone like the sun. Crease on my trousers was sharper than any knife. My shoes, well, you could see the acne on your face in the reflection!

And so, every morning I would leave home on my bicycle at 0445 hrs, fully kitted out.

45 minutes of hard cycling, dodging stray dogs and the odd lorry.

I'd be the first to arrive at the hanger and wait for the instructor to arrive at about 0545 hrs. Then, I'd clean the glider and the hanger.

Preflight checks would follow.

At 0615 hrs we'd push the Rohini glider out and take it to the take off point. Since I was generally the earliest bird, I got the first sortie.

On the instructor's command from the cockpit, I'd clamber in and strap up.

Kuldeep and a helper would hold each wingtip to balance the glider on its one wheel.

The cable would be attached to the nose. This was a 1200 m long steel cable attached at the other end of the airfield to a winch powered by an engine.

Pre-take-off checks done; we'd give the third helper a thumbs up whereupon he'd wave a green flag.

The winch operator would switch on the winch at the far end of the airfield. And, we'd begin the take-off run as the winch pulled our glider.

Soon the helpers let go because the glider was balanced on its wheel and running smoothly forward.

When ground speed hit around 50 km, we eased gently back on the joystick and the glider took off. As the winch continued to windup the cable, our altitude increased in the nose up position. At around 800 feet, at the instructor's command I leaned forward and pulled the cable release lever. When the cable fell away, the nose immediate dipped lower.

I simply loved the sudden sensation in my stomach as the nose of the Rohini fell downwards.

A correction with the stick and we were back on straight and level. From then on it was pure airmanship!

No engine and no cable. The glider was on its own.

We could only keep it in the air if we maintained airspeed and lift.

And so, the focused search for thermals, columns of warm air rising upwards.

A kettle[3], a group of circling eagles is the sure sign of a thermal. Clumps of trees, another indication.

We'd head for these. After catching a thermal the glider would gain lift and altitude.

Once we flew past an eagle slightly higher on our starboard side and closer to me because I was always in the righthand seat.

I still remember the eagle's puzzled look: what's this strange UFO doing in my airspace?!

Flying at about 1500 feet in a glider is pure joy!

Apart from the gentle swish of cool air rushing past the windscreen of our open cockpit, absolute silence and a peace that passeth understanding!

And then it happened once, and a couple of times more later.

After take-off, at about 400 feet I suddenly felt a snap-jerk and the nose fell sharply.

"Cable break my controls" my instructor, a seasoned glider pilot, Captain Subramanyam said calmly as he took over the controls from me.

The cable had snapped!

---

[3] *A group of birds of prey like eagles, hawks and vultures soaring on warm, rising air currents*

The glider lost airspeed suddenly, the nose dipped quickly, almost precipitously.

A stall loomed.

If we run out of airfield a crash is certain. It's an emergency!

Coolly, Capt. Subramanyam pushed the stick forward, avoided a stall (at about 48 km per hour the Rohini tends to stall, namely, lose lift to stay aloft), levelled out and then began a steep descent to land without batting an eyelid.

Supreme composure and skill in a tight situation. He simply followed the process.

Diagnose. Assess. Initiate corrective action. No panic. Allow skills and training to take over.

We suffered cable breaks several more times. Each time I learnt to follow the process. Invaluable life training!

This lesson has remained with me for a lifetime.

Anticipate problems and be prepared with a contingency plan-process. It's always going to be When, not if!

When an emergency hits, follow the process.

If a particular problem or emergency is not anticipated or is totally unexpected, simply revert to basics.

Stay calm. Diagnose, Assess, Initiate corrective action.

Debrief.

Learn.

Implement in the next iteration.

Cable breaks happen almost every day in every part of life. Do I react or do I respond?

Respond.

Follow the process.

SDAIDLI (Stay calm, Diagnose, Assess, Initiate Action, Debrief, Learn, Implement).

I'm eternally grateful to Sqn. Leader Springer and Capt. Subramanyam for the lessons I learnt from them.

Cable breaks can make the person, not break him or her!

6. Travails Of Captaincy

A booming voice rang out from beyond the sight screen. "Dixit has to be part of the team."

It was a command.

I looked for the source of that familiar voice.

There he was, my dear friend Vishwanath. Tall, hefty, rough Vishwanath.

He attracted arguments that somehow always managed to culminate in fisticuffs.

A few months ago, as we were practising on the tennis courts of the Sports Club of Gujarat, he got into it again!

A middling, mercurial tennis player, he was always intense about everything.

One of the boys wanted the court. Vishwanath wouldn't vacate because he'd arrived first.

One thing led to another and the boy made the mistake of shoving the big boy. And that was it. Viswanath punched him in the face.

With blood streaming from a broken nose he screamed, "Wait. I'm going to come back here with my big brother and his friends. I'll see that your legs are broken. I'm waiting right here. Bring big brother and his gang. We'll see who suffers broken legs".

Viswanath wasn't about to be cowed down.

I was watching all this from the corner of my eye while hitting tennis balls on the far court. I'd heard every word.

I knew there was going to be trouble.

Vishwanath had just beaten up the local bully's kid brother.

The big fella was quite the maverick. He was ever ready to explode. But he was also deeply loyal and affectionate.

The kind of person who'd stand by you no matter what. We shared a deep friendship.

He admired my tennis and I admired his courage. Viswanath looked around and saw me.

I stopped my practice and walked over to him. "You shouldn't have hit him.

But didn't you see that he shoved me first?

Yes, I did. You could've stayed cool and come over to my court and joined me. Why get into a fight over this?

Well, you know I'm not going to be quiet when someone, whoever, gets physical with me. In any case, let's see what he's going to do."

Viswanath wasn't perturbed at all.

I could see that he'd steeled himself for a real brawl.

This was my first real test of loyalty!

My best friend was facing grave danger. Was I going to abandon him?

"I don't agree with what you did. But I'm staying right here with you. Idiot. This has nothing to do with you.

It has everything to do with me, you moron. If it's your fight, its mine too". I wasn't going to let Vishwanath face the bullies alone.

There was no way I was going to abandon my friend.

And so, we waited. Dusk set in. All the other tennis players packed up and left. The two of us waited, with tennis rackets in hand.

If we were outnumbered, we could at least crack a few bones before we went down!

We waited and waited, until the evening dissolved into night. The bullies had lost nerve.

Nobody was coming.

Who wants to fight two tall, strong tennis players with rackets in hand! There was no sense in staying any longer.

Viswanath's gravelly voice interrupted my concentration on the court. He was right behind me.

"Say that again?

Dixit has to be in the college tennis team" he said with a finality.

Dixit was a dear common friend and an excellent tennis player.

At 17 years of age, I was Captain of the St. Xavier's College (Ahmedabad) tennis team and had won the University of Gujarat tennis title. As Captain of the University tennis team, I had played in the All India Inter University Tournament too. I was also amongst the Top 20 Promising Junior players in India (and No.1 Junior in Gujarat State) sent to the National Institute of Sports, Patiala for advanced coaching.

For the next year, my college entrusted me with the responsibility of selecting the team to represent St Xavier's in the University Tennis Tournament. I could choose anyone I thought fit, no questions asked.

That's why Viswanath was insisting that I select Dixit.

"Nath, there are better players who deserve to be in the team.

Maybe, but Dixit is our dear friend, especially yours. Shouldn't you give him preferential treatment?". Vishwanath was clearly exasperated.

He had a point, a very important consideration.

Shouldn't friendship count for something? What are friends for anyway? All kinds of thoughts raced through my mind.

Then, from the depths of my being Achan[4] and his principled life came to the fore.

And how could I ignore Appooppan (my paternal grandfather, Sadasya Thilakan TK Velupillai[5] and Valiachan (my maternal grandfather, K Kuttikrishna Menon[6]) and all that they stood for?

After all, I carried their genes and names (in my initials V K)! My spine stiffened.

There was no way I was going to bend my principles. For friendship, I was willing to give my life.

But merit was going to be my only criterion for selecting the team. "Nath, I'm sorry that's not the way it works on my watch.

---

[4] *V Madhavan Nair "Mali"*
[5] *Sadasya Thilakan TK Velupillai, statesman and author of Travancore State Manual*
[6] *Barrister K Kuttikrishna Menon, former Advocate General of Madras Presidency*

Yes, Dixit is my, our, dear friend. And yes, he's a damn good player. But there are others who're even better. My responsibility as the Captain is to select the very best team! And that's what I'm going to do.

"So, what're you going to do?" He was getting angry now.

"Here's what's going to happen. We're going to create a level playing field. Let's play a college selection tournament in which all of us, you, Dixit, me and all the others are going to play. The college team will comprise the Winner and Runner Up, the Top 2, of the tournament.

That's fair." Vishwanath seemed mollified!

That's when he grabbed me by the collar and yelled, "You goddamn fool! As University Champion it's your automatic right to be Captain of the college team. There's no need in hell for you to play a college tournament. Are you crazy?"

But I was never clearer and calmer.

"Nath, we're all friends for life. The rules apply equally to all of us. But on some basic principles I'm never ever going to compromise. If on that basis I lose a friendship, so be it. I'd rather lose a friend than violate my conscience."

We played the tournament. I won.

Atul Shah was runner up.

Dixit Desai didn't make the team.

I've never seen or heard from Vishwanath since we left college.

But it was Vishwanath's friendship and the travails of captaincy that gave me the opportunity to discover and cement my values.

And so, it has been throughout my life!

7. Loyola Days!

Plop…plop…plop…

I heard this strangely suggestive sound as I walked towards a room in 7th Block of the hostel in Loyola College, Madras (now Chennai). The sound grew louder as I got closer. I drew level with the doorway and glanced into the room.

A group of seniors were sitting in a circle. In the centre was a hapless fresher.

A ribbon was tied around his head.

A badminton racket drooped from his hand.

He was sitting on a bucket, more like in the bucket. Simulation of defecation!

His embarrassed voice was ringing along the corridor…. Plop... plop... The sound was, well, you get the drift!

This was (later) my dearest lifelong friend Shanky who'd just arrived for his First Year, B.A. Economics program.

He was being ragged by the seniors!

Then they saw me in the doorway and one of them came out to drag me in too.

But then he recognised me.

"Sorry sir" he mumbled and went right back where he came from.

The raggers were all final year degree students.

I had just joined the college as a Post Graduate student for my Master's in Economics.

So, there was no way a degree student could rag me! Protocol!

Shanky and I became thick pals.

Mostly because both of us played tennis on Court No. 1 of Loyola's 10 courts.

And partly because his father and my father were also very good friends and rivals on the tennis circuit in erstwhile Travancore State.

Loyola Hostel was a fun place filled with the smartest young men in the country.

Many, many of them were also preparing for the Civil Services and other tough competitive examinations.

So, the intellectual level of discussion, especially at dinner was extremely high.

Wit and repartee were currency of survival!

If your guard was down for a moment, well, you'd get hammered with sarcasm and satire!

People like BS and Muskie were the stuff of legend!

BS (Bull Shit) Nair was famous and still is, unmatched for irreverent humour!

And Muskie (a.k.a Gadai) was in a class of his own. He wore soda glasses and regularly walked full tilt into glass doors!

Individually each was a riot. Imagine the two of them teaming up. Loyola Hostel had a strict rule.

At 8.25 pm the First Bell would ring and at 8.30 pm, the Second. After Second Bell you HAD to be in your own room.

If you were caught wandering outside, there would be hell to pay, including expulsion from the Hostel.

Warden was an evil presence, forever lurking in the shadows to catch an errant wanderer.

The Rule was to ensure that the boys were tied to their books. Fat chance!

Post Graduate students were of course exempt. But naturally, there was great pride in breaking the Rule!

BS & Muskie concocted a diabolical plan to shatter the hostel's peace and quiet.

And thumb a nose at Warden to boot.

At exactly 9.30 pm BS would set off crackers at the far end of the hostel campus while Muskie did the same right in front of Warden's room.

And both would melt into the darkness and creep back to their respective rooms. The plan was set, watches were synchronised, the die was cast.

Both took positions at their designated spots.

At 9.25 pm crackers exploded from BS's location. Warden rushed out.

And caught Muskie red handed, lit match and crackers in hand. Muskie was flung out from the hostel for six whole months.

To this day mystery persists about why the crackers ignited 5 minutes ahead of schedule from BS's location.

But suspicion lingers.

Once, a group of us were gossiping in Sunny's room long after Second Bell, of course.

We were enjoying some hot chocolate that Sunny had received from home. The electric kettle was being put to good use.

Suddenly a mildly offensive smell permeated the cramped room.

Then, smoke and a strange sizzling, crackling sound with a glow attached.

Shanky's hair was on fire!

He'd been leaning against an exposed wire from Sunny's kettle! Pandemonium!

Water bottles were emptied on Shanky's head and the situation was brought under control only just!

A few minutes later we froze and held our breaths. We could hear Warden's heavy tread trudge past. No damage done.

Shanky's hair had a funny smell, though.

No tale from Loyola Hostel is complete without Muskie's pet egg.

He had an old biscuit tin in his room. It was three fourth full of rice.

Within the grains of rice nestled an egg. Muskie's pet!

The nest egg sat in the rice for nearly two full years.

Until Jayaram broke it just before Muskie's the MA final exams.

The stink was so bad that Muskie couldn't even go near his room, let alone stay in it.

Apparently, the egg's metamorphosis into stink had a lot to do with Muskie's super performance in the exams!

Muskie is short for Mosquito.

Rumour has it that Gadai used to sit for hours with a notebook open. Waiting for a mosquito to fly between the pages.

And then the notebook would be snapped shut.

A notebook plastered with mosquitos was found in his room after Muskie graduated.

8. Peace That Passeth Understanding

Ma (Mother) Ganga flows in divine majesty from the Himalayas into the Arabian Sea.

She's quite literally the mother of the Hindu heritage.

Some 25 kilometres north of the holy town of Rishikesh, on the highway to Badrinath, Ma Ganga hosts an ancient cave on her banks.

A cave like no other.

The cave in which Sage Vasishtha, one of the Saptarishis (7 great sages) meditated and therefore, sanctified, aeons ago.

Vasishta Gufa (cave).

Swami Purushottamanandaji too used to meditate in this cave in the 1950s.

He'd gone into Devabhumi (land of the Gods) as the pristine wilderness of the Himalayas is known…far, far away from his home in Central Travancore.

As a young monk practising austerities, he received not just knowledge and wisdom but also many Siddhis (yogic powers).

Such is his spiritual grace and potency that he's been seen and felt in and around the Vasistha Gufa long after he'd shed his mortal body.

Amidst the ruggedly beautiful serenity of the Himalayan mountains, on the banks of Ma Ganga, Swamiji set up his sacred Ashram more than 70 years ago.

Right outside Vasishta Gufa.

A small, isolated sanctuary in the middle of the forbidding forest. We arrived at the Ashram around 3.30 pm in July 2011.

It was quiet, very quiet.

The Ashram Manager, RK Mishra (Mishraji) welcomed us with kindness.

When he found that we were from Kochi he ushered us into the presence of the Guru.

Head of the Ashram. Swami Chaitanyanandaji.

An octogenarian brahmachari (celibate monk) in saffron. Brimming with affection.

He knew about Achan[7] and his family. He was an admirer of Achan's work.

"Mali's son" is the proud introduction that I've worn as a badge of honour all my life.

So, naturally, Swamiji extended the greatest kindness and hospitality to us. Mishraji brought us hot tea and Glucose biscuits.

Radha and I sat at his feet and listened with rapt devotion to the stories he told about his own direct Guru, Swami Purushottamanandaji.

---

[7] *My revered father V Madhavan Nair "Mali"*

Swamiji asked Radha to sing and she did, receiving his copious blessings. And then Mishraji opened the gate to Vasistha Gufa and took us inside.

Once we were within the Gufa he left us so we could pray and meditate. The Gufa covered us with a thick cloak of pitch darkness.

Darkness that stretched into infinity, into deep space.

Lightened by a small, single oil lamp casting an otherworldly glow into timelessness.

We sat down and slipped into meditation.

After about 20 minutes I felt Radha leaving softly. I was alone.

Within the bowels of this primordial cave. In deep silence, so deep that I could hear it.

Crackling with vibrations from a Divine Presence. My entire being was transported into another realm. I came to after a full 45 minutes.

I'd traveled across time and space and returned to temporal reality. Everything within me changed.

Couldn't fathom how, but I knew I'd changed.

I emerged from the Gufa, my eyes adjusting to the fading sunlight. We met Swamiji again and thanked him for his gracious welcome. "We'll be back, Swamiji."

"Yes, I know. We'll meet again." He was sure that we'll return.

Next morning we had planned to go whitewater rafting in the hurrying waters of MaGanga.

We headed out after a late breakfast.

After driving for more than an hour there was no sign of the rafting centre. We looked around but just couldn't find our bearings.

Had we passed the place? Should we drive forward or retrace? "Let's go forward for a few more minutes."

"Ok, let's stop here and look for someone to ask for directions". I stepped out of the car.

Not a single soul in sight. Not even a passing vehicle.

I glanced down. And there it was. Amidst the trees. A familiar place. Vasishta Gufa Ashram!

We'd arrived at the spot on the highway, just above the Ashram.

I don't quite know how we managed to get lost and then stop at this very location. It was a pretty straight-forward drive from Rishikesh to the whitewater rafting centre.

How did we return to this point?

Something or someone was pulling us towards the Ashram.

"Since we're here, let's go down to the Ashram and meet Swamiji again," I said.

So down the steps we went. It was 1215 pm.

The Ashram was deserted. Pin drop silence.

We stood around in the open ground, uncertain about what to do.

"Madhav Mohan Ji, aayiye, aayiye (please come)". Mishraji's warmth laden voice rang out.

"Come, Swamiji is waiting for you." I thought he was just being polite.

Mishraji led us into a small dining room set along the side of the Ashram. Half a dozen people sat on the floor with plates in front of them.

Lunch was about to be served.

And there was Swamiji, seated on a slightly raised wooden platform. There were two plates placed right next to him.

He greeted us with a beautiful smile.

"I was waiting for you. See, I've kept two places for you. Come, let's have lunch together".

We were dumbfounded.

How did we end up here when we had no intention to return so soon? And, more amazingly, how did he know we'd be back today?

He was so sure that he'd laid out two plates, waiting for us to join him for lunch!

There simply was no explanation. Lunch was simple and delightful.

We spent a little more time with Swamiji.

He regaled us with stories and experiences …everything was about his Guru, Swami Purushottamanandaji.

Swami Chaityanyanandaji had devoted his entire life to Guru Seva (serving the Guru), to furthering the Guru's work and popularising his writings.

As we took leave after this wondrous reunion, Swamiji handed me a few books.

"These are some of my Gurudev's books. I'm sure you'll find them useful. And, by the way, please know that there is always a room ready for you here".

We took leave after seeking his blessings.

I was struck by the serenity and peace radiating from this great Swamiji, his Gurudev, the Gufa and the Ashram.

As we climbed the steps back to our car on the highway the phrase "peace that passeth understanding, peace that passeth understanding" flooded my consciousness.

As though someone was whispering into my soul.

Even as we boarded the car and left, the phrase was playing over and over again within me.

A few minutes later I opened one of the books that Swamiji gifted to me. The first words that my eyes saw as I opened a random page stunned me! "The peace that passeth understanding!"

How did this statement originating from Philippians 4:7 of the Bible, describing a divine, unshakable inner calm insert itself into my consciousness just before I opened the book to see this exact phrase?

And that too, in Swami Purushottamanandaji's book at that exact location in those serene environs?

I don't know.

All I know is that I'd been given a priceless treasure. A cave to return to in turbulent times within me.

9. Reckoning On The Tennis Court

The red hardcourt of Rama Varma Club Kochi was baking in the late afternoon heat.

The tram lines and baselines were freshly marked with white chalk. I was playing the most intense set of singles tennis in my life.

Across the court Mostafa was huffing and puffing like a steam engine. He was panting uncontrollably in a desperate effort to get to the ball.

Sweat was pouring out of him in a torrent. The score was 3-0 in my favour.

And I was about to begin my service game. That's when Dr Paulose made a noisy entrance!

He was (still is) my long-term tennis partner and dearest friend. A much older player, a seasoned doctor by profession.

Amongst the wiliest, deadliest players ever on a tennis court.

A couple of years earlier he'd taken a reigning India No. 3 to the brink of defeat.

He'd narrowly missed converting a match point.

Equipped with an innocuous looking pat-ball service and unimpressive ground strokes.

But he could place the ball with pinpoint accuracy and consistency. He was nothing short of a silent assassin on a tennis court!

We knew each other's game, body language and thoughts like the back of our respective hands.

Paulose was nothing else but loud. His guffaw brought every game alive. When he saw the scowl of intensity on my face, he stopped short.

"What is it, Madhav?" he asked with concern. "I've never seen you so serious."

I grimaced and indicated that I'd explain later. And began to serve.

Ace down the middle. 15 love.

Ace, this time wide off the backhand. 30 love.

Ace wide off the forehand. 40 love.

Hard, fast serve into the body. Game, 4-0.

Mostafa's turn to serve. Drop.

Lob.

Forehand corner. Backhand corner.

Short forehand cross court.

Deep backhand down the line Sliced backhand cross court.

Gentle forehand down the line near the service court.

And so it went.

Mostafa had to scamper back and forth. Forwards and backwards.

Side to side.

No respite.

No mercy.

15 love, 30 love, 40 love, game

4 love, then 5 love and finally, game and set, 6 love; 6-0. I had punished him mercilessly.

Without dropping a single point.

I had deliberately toyed with him, teasing the ball away from him so that he'd have to chase it before sending it back shakily over the net.

Every point was dragged out to inflict maximum physical exertion. It was a 24 point, 6 love set.

Utter and total humiliation.

By the end of it he could barely stand, such was his exhaustion. He staggered to the net to shake my hand.

I had barely broken a sweat.

Watching from the spectator's area, Paulose was speechless.

I put my racket down and sat next to him. And told him the story.

5 years ago, I had borrowed money from a loan shark. At about 30 % per annum.

The kind of lender who would break your legs if you didn't repay on time. I was beginning my journey as an entrepreneur in an unheard-of business. Computer education and software development.

Circa 1984.

Mine was a first-generation business in a new field without any chance of bank finance

We were eternally short of working capital. And so, I missed the repayment date.

A week later, the lender turned up at my home. Mostafa.

He abused my family, including my revered father. Unforgettable, unforgivable, in my book anyway. Of course, I repaid the loan with Herculean effort.

And so, it was the very same Mostafa who chanced upon me at the club that afternoon.

He fancied himself as a tennis player. He'd never seen me play.

"How about a set, Madhav?"

"Certainly! Come, let's play," This was my opportunity!

Repayment, with interest was exacted for humiliation. In the most proper way.

On a field of play.

It was a complete, satisfying reckoning on the tennis court.

10. Imposter!

I walked into a Board Room reeking of scepticism, unsure of what to expect.

Who's this young imposter? How did he get here?

What strings did he pull and who's his godfather?

We'll soon see the stuff he's made of, or most likely, the lack of it. His pathetic capabilities will be laid bare for sure soon.

I could hear their thoughts. And feel the disdain.

The MD and top management of the State Bank of Travancore were waiting.

For the new Director to arrive.

Arguably, one of the youngest ever directors of a large Public Sector Bank in India.

Age, 41.

Me!

I had the distinct feeling that I was out of my depth.

After accepting the mandatory bouquet of flowers, I sat down at the table. The high table of Indian banking.

I looked around.

Every one of them was at least 15 years older to me. Some even older.

The top team of the bank was a formidable lot, each with nearly 3 decades of experience.

Most of them were former Probationary Officers who joined the bank after the toughest selection program; a process that eliminated all but the creme de la creme of young talent in India.

I too had joined the State Bank of India as a Probationary Officer, at age 23.

If I had remained in the Bank, the people in that room would have treated me like a lesser form of life.

I'd not even be allowed onto the floor, let alone the Board Room!

But I had quit after just 3 years and lived out of my wits for a long time now. I'd refused to be seduced by the monthly pay check!

Without much ado the Board Meeting commenced.

My very first meeting as a Director. The Agenda was mountainous.

30 files, each containing hundreds of pages of arcane banking matters. From loan proposals to human resource issues.

Legal tangles and commercial wrangles.

Facts, figures, concepts, policies, strategies, action plans, performance reporting.

It was all in the Agenda.

Everything to do with thousands of employees, millions of depositors, and billions worth of deposits and loans.

Backed up by the most detailed documentation you can imagine. Thousands of pages of excruciating detail.

Absolutely mind boggling. Overwhelming!

How could I cope with this kind of a load?

Application of mind dictated that Directors had to study every comma and full stop thoroughly. Their decisions affected the entire financial and banking ecosystem.

How can such a young Director handle such an onerous responsibility? Imposter! He doesn't deserve to be here.

I could hear them think.

I knew that I'd be on probation!

The jury was out on my abilities.

I had prepared diligently for that first meeting. It was a trial by fire.

Discussions were intense. Points of view were divergent.

Each Director was a leader and expert.

How could I make my views clear in such an environment, let alone contribute!

But help was at hand.

"I agree with Mr. Madhav Mohan. His idea about training programs for the Credit Department is definitely worth exploring".

Mr. Narayanamurthy was amongst the most sought after Chartered Accountants in the country.

As the longest serving Director his views were the most influential.

The kindness and credibility of Mr. Narayanamurthy had smoothened my entry into the Board.

I felt an immediate change in the attitude of everyone around the table. A newbie was made to feel comfortable and accepted!

How could I not be motivated and inspired to give my best? My efforts intensified for every meeting thereafter.

For 6 years.

The preparation paid rich dividends.

My comfort level improved with each meeting.

Soon, I was nominated to the Executive Committee (EC), the powerful subcommittee of the Board of Directors.

Managing Director (MD) was the CEO of the Bank.

But it was EC (which included MD) which made all the most important decisions.

Over the next year I'd put my head down and digest the Agenda for EC Meetings

Every 3 weeks.

Nose to the grindstone.

Reading, struggling to understand. Striving for clarity of thought.

With practice I could read through and understand thousands of pages. In about 4 torturous hours of continuous, concentrated study.

Exhausting!

Over time I discovered that I could remember facts and details.

That's how I learned the importance and value of consistency and discipline.

It was a great opportunity to contribute by making life altering decisions.

Like supporting the Cochin International Airport Ltd. despite poor financials because supply would create demand; thereby boosting regional economic development.

With trepidation!

Was I making too risky a decision?

Throwing the book at an errant General Manager even though he had a close relationship with my family.

With pain and regret that I couldn't help him. Avoiding blandishments from prospective borrowers.

Not succumbing to political pressure and refusing to sanction loans to a fiscally imprudent state government.

Introducing information technology on a massive scale. Strengthening recoveries.

Sanctioning big ticket loans.

Helping reduce Non-Performing Assets to a tenth of what it was.

I had joined State Bank of India (SBI) as a starry-eyed young probationer.

Here I was on the Board of one of its largest subsidiaries as SBI's own nominee.

And officiating as Chairman of the Bank to conduct an Extraordinary General Body Meeting.

Unbelievable.

I did the best I could.

The rest of it wasn't in my control at all.

For me, serving on the Board of State Bank of Travancore was the privilege of a lifetime.

The privilege was compounded because my grandfather, Sadasya Thilakan TK Velupillai had been its first Legal Advisor over a half century ago.

The imposter had survived, barely.

11. What's In A Word?

That's not correct!

Her voice was a mixture of condescension and impatience. "What's not correct, Nancy?" I didn't think I said anything wrong.

Nancy and I were part of a group assigned to do a study of the Chilean economy.

It was part of a course we were taking at Thunderbird[8]. Perhaps she thought I was not up to speed on the assignment. Or that I had difficulty communicating in English.

I was after all, an oddity in an American University, especially as far afield as Arizona.

An Indian in Glendale, Arizona in 1981? Talk about a rare species!

Did Indians speak English?

"How come your English is so good?" I was asked countless times.

India was a far-off land of stray, skeletal cows wandering on dusty roads.

From being the richest geography in the world some 500 years ago, it was systematically reduced to penury.

---

[8] *American Graduate School of Management (also known informally as Thunderbird), now known as Thunderbird School of Global Management, Arizona State University, USA*

An ancient land impoverished by British colonial rule.

In such a milieu how could anyone be fluent in English?

Hardly anyone on my campus knew that the education system in India, even then, despite its shortcomings, was still world class.

Not only did we have felicity, many of us actually thought in English too. Because we were taught the language from the time, we were 5 years old!

In fact, we learnt several languages. But for me, English was the medium of instruction right from primary school upwards.

"That word is not correct. Which word?

"What did you say, Madhav? Something like liaison." Nancy was exasperated.

"Oh, you mean liaise? I was just saying that we should liaise with the other groups to make sure that we're on the right track."

"Ah, yeah, that's the one. I don't think that's correct though. It's not a word in English."

"Oh yes, Nancy, it's very much a word that exists in English. Maybe not used much, but certainly part of the lexicon."

"No way, that's not true!"

"You wanna bet, Nancy?"

"Yes, yes!"

"Ok, could you check the dictionary?"

"Of course, I'm gonna go to our library on campus right now and see," she said and hurried off.

Nancy was such an earnest gem!

About an hour later she caught up with me in the Cafeteria.

"Nancy! Have a seat. Can I get you anything? Coke, coffee, a sandwich maybe?"

"I'll have a Coke, thanks".

I ran up to the counter and bought a Coke and some pastries too. "I was right. Liaise doesn't exist. You cooked it up!"

"No, no, Nancy, much as I would've liked to, I didn't cook it up! It is a bonafide word in the English language."

"How come I couldn't find it in the dictionary?"

"Maybe you didn't look in the right dictionary. Since it's not a common usage some dictionaries may not carry it. But that doesn't mean liaise doesn't exist in the language."

"Ok, Madhav. I'll go down to the Phoenix Public Library and check it out". Nancy was nothing if not dead serious about everything she did.

Next afternoon, after classes were done for the day, we rendezvoused at the Cafeteria.

She had a distinctly chastened look. "Well, Nancy?"

"You were right. I found it in a couple of dictionaries at the Phoenix Public Library. Liaise means forming a liaison, to communicate and make contact (with); it's a verb, used without object; a form of liaison, liaised, liaisoning. I learned something! Thank you, Madhav!"

Nancy was relieved that the mystery of the unfamiliar word was solved. From then on, Nancy and I became friends for life.

What's in a word, you might ask. A lifetime of friendship!

12. Heartbroken!

That's that... Computer?

This is an electronic device that can cutout mistakes, speed up tasks and eliminate the drudgery of repetitive tasks.

Oh no, that's not at all suitable for Indian conditions.

No one knew or cared or even wanted to consider the possibility that computers were relevant and necessary.

This newfangled technology was sure to throw vast multitudes out of work.

As if most of our people were already employed and enjoying great prosperity!

It was just too much of a hot political potato. Much more so in communist ruled Kerala.

Circa 1982 in India.

It was like banging my head against a granite wall.

The idea that computers were India's path to prosperity.

Because of our education, and innate ability to think logically and innovate. My weird ideas just after returning from study in the US had no takers at all.

Hardware was nails, fasteners, hammers and the likes, what you bought in a store.

Software? Some kind of stuffed toy?

Programming? Creating entertainment schedules? Well, you get the drift!

I proposed the idea that computer programming should be taught to young children.

And got derision, sarcasm and contempt.

Look at this guy, returns from the US with unworkable ideas, quits a prestigious, steady job with State Bank of India and is now literally on the streets.

Showered with pity.

Bank after bank turned me down. Investors ridiculed me.

Never felt more alone or useless.

And then a dear friend offered to invest. He brought along a big businessman.

They would invest, have a controlling interest and I would implement my idea.

How else could I get any resources?

After all I was a first-generation entrepreneur with no resources at all.

I spent many, many hours in consultation with Justice Nampoodiripad, a storied retired High Court Judge.

He was known, feared even, for his extreme honesty and integrity. His deep wisdom and loving encouragement were my refuge.

We were hammering out a legal document encompassing a new age of technology.

Soon a pathbreaking agreement emerged.

An agreement between our company and schools.

The company would provide computer hardware, software and teachers; the school would provide an air-conditioned classroom and collect fees from children.

By 1984, we were teaching BASIC programming to over 1000 school children.

In 5 schools, including several public schools in Ooty (now, Udhagamandalam).

Revenue was pouring in!

Meanwhile, one of the Directors in the company wanted to employ the son of his employee.

The boy was just 19!

He'd not studied beyond high school but had a diploma in automobile engineering.

Essentially, he was wasting his life. Smart, but no skills, no direction. Kishore.

I took him on as an understudy, happily. I was all of 28 years old!

From, figuring out computers, understanding business, dressing properly and conducting himself with grace, I left nothing out.

He was a quick learner. Too quick.

Soon, we entrusted the entire Ooty operation to him because his family had deep roots there.

Virtually all our revenue came out of this geography.

One fateful day, Nandan, my faithful assistant, made a phone call to me from Ooty.

"Kishore is threatening me. He has goondas[9] lined up and they are forcing me to leave town or else. They're also saying that they'll kill you if you set foot in Ooty again."

Quietly, he'd got every school to rewrite the contracts in his name. All the revenue now flowed into his account.

He'd taken all the costly hardware, software and the best computer teachers.

In one fell swoop he'd misappropriated the entire business.

The business model, revenue stream, assets, intellectual property, everything but everything was purloined.

Products of my mind and creativity. Stolen.

Just like that.

With the connivance of my friend the investor and his friend the other investor.

Disbelief and hurt can hardly describe my feelings.

But I decided then and there that I'll be better, not bitter.

Someone thought they could destroy me they had another think coming! For the next few years my life, and that of the family, was a nightmare.

---

[9] *Gangsters*

Filled with humiliation and near bankruptcy. Warding off toxic thoughts and rough creditors. Pain and penury.

Holding steady, building from scratch minus, polishing my skills. Under fire from every direction.

Staying on the path, clutching my values. They say Karma can't be denied.

And so, it wasn't.

He'd cheated my former investors too, the ones who had connived with him.

Some 2 decades later, he was arrested on criminal charges and sent to jail.

The multimillion-dollar business that the understudy had built on valueless foundations collapsed.

I could never gloat.

So long ago my sincerity had been repaid with cunning and deceit. I was sad that it all had to come to this.

I'd been violated.

And betrayed.

Forgiven? Maybe.

Forgotten?

Never.

Heartbroken… still.

13. Halcyon Days

A soft knock on the door. 6 am, 3rd October 1978.

"Good morning, Sir. Bed tea, sir".

I opened the door, groggy after a long train journey from Kochi to Chennai.

A steaming cup of chai with Parle Glucose biscuits served by a smiling butler.

State Bank Staff College, Hyderabad.

The 1978 Batch of State Bank of India (SBI) Probationary Officers had arrived at the lush, plush campus of the Bank's prestigious training centre for Officers.

A clutch of excitable probationers.

Young women and men full of promise, more women than men. The best and brightest in the country.

Handpicked after a rigorous selection-elimination process by the premier bank of the country.

The group from which the Bank's future leadership was expected to emerge.

Many from this cohort would later pass the Union Public Service Commission exams and become members of the Indian Foreign Service, Indian Administrative Service, Indian Police

Service and other Central Services and go on to become leaders of the "Steel Frame of India"[10].

Soon the butler returned to take our clothes for ironing and shoes for shining.

The Bank's probationers were being treated like royalty!

A proper breakfast with gleaming cutlery and waiters in attendance. And then we found ourselves in the Seminar/Training Hall.

A seasoned, senior officer walked in at 9 am sharp. A round of introductions followed.

We got a brief history of SBI and how it had evolved from the old Imperial Bank.

To make us make us feel comfortable he tried to introduce some levity. "Do you know the SBI definition of customer?".

Some eager beavers raised their hands. None of them got it right.

"You should know. The SBI definition of customer, is in Hindi, 'kasht se jo marta hai usay kashtmar kehate hain'[11]"

One who dies of kasht, difficulty/suffering is called kashtmar, customer. There was much mirth around the room.

Wow, the Bank has such a sense of humour.

Later we were assigned to toil in branches on the front lines of Indian banking.

---

[10] *The professional administration of the Government of India..and its States*
[11] *Kasht in Hindi means difficulty/suffering. Marta means dies. So, kasht se jo marta hai usay kashtmar kahte hain literally means "one who dies of difficulty is called a customer"!*

Only then did it dawn on us that the senior officer's joke was actually the truth!

After an hour or so a hand went up. "Sir, can we take a water break?

Of course, young man. Do you want to make water or take water?" If this was the level of humour in the Bank, God help us!

We found solace in mutual good-natured leg pulling.

10 days later we were moved from the luxurious Staff College to the more pedestrian Staff Training Centre.

It was an old palace up in Banjara Hills, Hyderabad. Dark passages, musty old cavernous rooms.

Alcoves and balconies, some overlooking the entrance. Large makeshift bedrooms shared by 6 people.

Mosquito nets and magic carpets.

Women's quarters were just across the hallway. No locks, no moral policing.

Officers were expected to be 'responsible.' A dining hall, adjacent to the palace.

For the next 30 odd days this was our home.

Day and practically most nights, we were taught the fundamentals of banking.

Working in a dummy bank (the term for simulation in those days). Learning how to conduct transactions.

Writing vouchers, passing them. Posting in ledgers.

Tallying accounts.

Balancing the 'Clean Cash Book'. Running a Clearing House.

Dealing with bounced cheques.

Adding endless rows of numbers and get it wrong most of the time. Studying the Negotiable Instruments Act.

Reading the voluminous Bank's Book of Instructions and endless circulars. Hard work!

Through it all the fun and frolic continued.

One evening, CM and I saw the women go into the dining hall for dinner. We laid a trap for them.

We positioned ourselves on a balcony just above the entrance to the palace.

And waited for them to return after dinner. Mid November cold!

A bucket of water was at hand, ready and waiting.

When they passed directly beneath us, cold water rained down on them. Squeals of indignation! Shake, shiver and shudder.

Giggles, hushed voices, then silence. But I knew something was brewing.

And then it was bedtime.

All of us were fast asleep, tired after all the excitement and work. A soft rustling snapped me out of my sleep.

I lay motionless trying to figure out the source of the noise. My eyes adjusted to the darkness.

And then I saw the shadowy figures…

The 5 batchmates who I had literally poured cold water on. All in night clothes.

Whispering.

Suppressed titters.

They were out for revenge for the drenching.

I jumped out of bed, switched on the light and locked the bedroom door from inside.

The girls were trapped! And all the guys woke up.

5 of them, officers all, in nighties, in the men's bedroom at 2 am! We nearly died of laughter.

They were caught red-handed with toothpaste and boot polish in their hands.

Intended retribution to smear paste and polish on our faces while we slept.

And then sneak off to sneer at us at breakfast next morning.

"Girls, girls! If you wanted to spend the night with us all you needed to do was ask. You didn't have to sneak into our room like this. Please stay, you're welcome anytime!"

The five of them rushed to the door, unlocked it in a jiffy and fled for their lives.

Breakfast next morning was great fun. The girls averted their eyes.

Of course, we plonked ourselves right next to them with fully laden plates. "So, how about tonight?"

Embarrassment maximum, blushes that lit up the room. It was a sight for the ages!

Soon the month of training was up.

We had to put up an entertainment show at the valedictory program. The Bank's brass would be present.

So, naturally, we decided to put up a weird skit, Shakespeare's Julius Caesar with a twist.

The acting and dialogue were pure ad-libbing, improv to the limit.

I was Caesar fated to be done in by Brutus. I was pushed to the ground by Brutus.

His knife was drawn.

That's when Lady Macbeth wanders on to the stage with a butter knife dripping ketchup.

A member of the Praetorian Guard, with a bedsheet for a cloak, taps her on the shoulder.

"Hey baby, you're in the wrong play. Yours is down the road". Macbeth makes a fuss wanting to be included in "this" play.

In the confusion I grab the knife from Brutus and stab him. "You too, Caesar," he cries as he falls to the ground.

Curtains fall.

Roaring laughter and wholesome applause. Banking thereafter was pretty exciting, if dry!

But those days in Staff College and Staff Training Centre…

…they were the halcyon days!

14. Sensei

Sridar Theatre predominantly screened English movies.

All the classics found a welcoming audience starved for international fare.

Every movie played to packed house.

Young men in those days, mid 1970s, hardly had an outlet for their energy. That's when Enter The Dragon hit the screens across India.

Bruce Lee.

The new God!

Awestruck audiences gaped with disbelief his speed and power. Could it be real?

Or was it all "camera tricks" lingering doubts.

But everyone desperately wanted to believe their eyes. Lightning speed compounded by brute force.

Silken moves and extraordinary flexibility.

Superhuman strength.

I couldn't even begin to describe the experience. Neither could the multitudes.

The crowd that exited after was not just excited. Everyone exhibited machismo, maximum.

The atmosphere cracked with electricity. Whoever saw the movie came out transformed. I can achieve anything!

Such was Bruce Lee's impact. I recognised the truth.

Tennis was in my blood…but martial arts was my soul. A burning desire to learn martial arts was ignited.

I began to read and look around for a class. If only I could find a Master!

A couple of years later I saw an innocuous ad in the paper. Master Kuppusamy from Malaysia invites students to learn Karate. I went to Usha Tourist Home in Kochi as soon as I could.

The receptionist in the nondescript hotel directed me to room on the ground floor.

I knocked with nervous anticipation. "Come".

I opened the door gingerly and stepped inside.

A dark, wiry young man was lounging shirtless in a pair of shorts. He was just a few years older than me.

One look and I knew.

I'd found my Sensei[12].

There was something indescribable about him.

Maybe terrifying strength beneath soft words and gentle behaviour. That was my first lesson.

True capabilities don't need to be broadcast by brash behaviour. Black belts don't reveal their capabilities.

---

[12] *Respectful term used to address a teacher, master or indeed someone who has attained high proficiency in any field. The word literally means "One who came before" from Sen = Before and Sei = Life in Japanese.*

Unless absolutely unavoidable. Then, settle the issue with one blow.

No arguments, no justifications, no theatrics. Just swift, fearless, decisive action.

Only when needed. Like a deadly Katana[13].

To be removed from its 'Saya', sheath, only in the direst circumstances. Once removed, behead the enemy.

Like the Gurkha's Khukri has to draw blood if it's out of its 'Dap or Daab' scabbard.

You couldn't tangle with Sensei.

A simple, uneducated man from Kuala Lumpur.

Embodiment of the warrior ethos. Honed by years of austere discipline. His Karate was sublime.

As a Sensei, he was unparalleled. Gentle but tough as nails.

As a Sensei, he was unparalleled. Gentle, encouraging but demanding the highest standards.

Such was his fame that at one point he had as many as 10,000 students I was amongst his very first students in this part of the country (Kerala). And so it was that I would be among the fire arrive at the Dojo[14]. Sweeping and cleaning the Dojo was the first order of business.

---

[13] *Traditional long curved sword used two handed by Samurai warriors; symbolises the warrior class and Bushido (The Way of The Warrior); sharp enough to slice effortlessly through enemies; highly valued not only as a weapon but also as a work of art*
[14] *Refers to a hall or space where martial arts are practiced; can be applied to any place dedicated to learning, spiritual practice, discipline or training; "Do means way or path and "Jo" means place in Japanese ; so, Dojo literally means place of the way."*

Humility.

Dignity of labour.

Don't give up, don't give in.

Valuable lessons all, learnt from the Dojo. Bruce Lee had led me to Sensei.

Once he asked me to provide commentary during a public Karate demonstration.

A remote town in Kerala.

A dark night lit up by dozens of tube lights. A smallish stage.

And hundreds of curious spectators. What is this Karatta or Karate?

Is it like Kalaripayattu[15]? Strange uniforms!

And stranger movements.

This is a 'Kata', I explained over the sound system.

A systematic set of movements blocks, punches, kicks.

All delivered with deadly force against imagined opponents.

Every single movement and blow had a designated objective to strike and disable the adversary[16].

---

[15] *Ancient martial art of Kerala*
[16] *Bunkai..the Japanese term for effects/impact/objective of each movement in a Kata..bunkai is the key to unlocking the hidden techniques and wisdom within a kata, making it an indispensable part of Karate training for both self-defense and deeper martial arts understanding. Its the practical application of every movement..practised endlessly to be used seamlessly in actual combata*

Senior students had demonstrated Katas and breaking techniques.

Blocks of ice, many tiles, bricks, all broken by punches and kicks with bare hands and feet.

"Now, dear friends, let's welcome Sensei Kuppusamy. You're about to experience a feat like no other."

My own excitement was palpable over the mike. A hush fell over the audience.

They had heard about this great Sensei and seen the posters.

Sensei stepped on to the stage in his off-white canvas 'Gi'[17]. A frayed black belt was tied impeccably around his waist.

Frayed because it'd been worn for thousands of hours.

A senior student placed an iron bar between two cement blocks. Sensei was attempting to break the bar with a Shuto knife hand.

It was a striking technique using the side of the hand opposite to the thumb.

Sensei took his position in Kiba Dachi horse stance and inhaled deeply. Then he simulated the blow in slow motion once.

Then a second time. And a third.

The crowd was beginning to get restless. I was extremely nervous.

Firstly, the bar was a good 3 inches in diameter.

---

[17] *Traditional garment ..uniform..worn during Karate practice..literally, "clothing" or "outfit"*

Just too thick, how can it be broken with a bare hand? Secondly, how will the crowd react if there's a glitch? What if the bar doesn't break?

Will Sensei's reputation be ruined? What a fool I was!

Sensei's hand moved with lightning speed… and struck the bar with full force.

Thud.

The bar was intact.

A sigh from the audience.

A second blow, faster, harder. Thud.

No joy, the bar hadn't even bent. Then a third blow.

A fourth and a fifth.

"Sensei, please stop. The bar's too thick. Your hand will break". He wasn't listening.

His face told the story.

He was in a different dimension.

None of us could reach him not me, not the audience… no one. Titters from the assemblage.

A series of Shuto strikes followed.

I counted about **8** more blows, each harder than the other. Sensei's entire being was concentrated on the Knife Hand. On the 13th blow the bar broke, clean in two.

A roar went up from the crowd. They surged onto the stage.

He was lifted high in the air.

And carried through the town on adoring shoulders.

There, in that remote town.

Cynicism had turned into hero worship.

I'd just caught a glimpse of the infinite capabilities of a clean, disciplined being.

The legend of Sensei Kuppusamy was born. Sensei!

15. Sojourn in Salzburg

Commissioned in 1736 by Prince Archbishop Anton von Firmian. An exemplar of Rococo architecture.

In Salzburg, Austria. Birthplace of Mozart.

Hometown of the world-famous Salzburg Festival of opera, Western Classical music and theatre.

A beacon of art and culture. Schloss Leopoldskron.

The quaint castle where the movie, "Sound of Music" was shot. Beautiful images of the Leopoldskroner Weiher, the Leopoldskron Pond. And the grounds.

Where Julie Andrews danced with the Von Trapp kids. While Untersberg Mountain looked on with indulgence. Etched in memories of a beautiful time.

Enriched by snatches of unforgettable songs, "Do re mi" and "My Favourite Things."

Now, home of The Salzburg Global Seminar.

Where former and future policy makers, Ambassadors, Prime Ministers even, came together for intellectual discourse.

Session 294 of the Seminar was underway.

Economies in Transition: The Role of The Private Sector (Feb 29-March 7 1992).

Some 50 odd economists from around the world had congregated at the Schloss Leopoldskron.

To discuss, debate and learn the nuances of economic transition. From state domination to market domination.

Eminent economists including Dr Mahbub Haq (creator of the Human Development Index and former Finance Minister of Pakistan) shared their incredible insights as Members of the Faculty.

I was lucky and deeply privileged to be invited to attend as a full Fellow. During a break, I got an opportunity for a tete-a-tete with Dr Haq himself. We sat in an alcove on the ground floor of the Schloss.

He was a deeply humane genius with a mastery of economic policy that was breathtaking.

From him I learnt that policy is rubbish unless it actually helps improve the human condition.

The breadth and depth of the technical sessions at the Seminar helped me clarify many doubts and dilemmas.

One morning I had a couple of hours to myself.

I thought I'd take a drive around the picturesque town. So, I'd booked a cab to arrive at 0800 hrs.

Most cabs were Mercedes Benzs.

Cabbies were usually women, expert drivers all.

Just as I was leaving my room to go down to the lobby my phone rang. Someone wanted to check our schedule for the day.

At 0803 hrs I was down at reception. I looked around.

No cab. Strange!

Weren't Austrians and Germans legendary in terms of punctuality? "I'm waiting for my cab; it was supposed to be here at 0800 hrs".

The receptionist smiled at me with condescension.

"She was here at 0759 hrs, waited 2 minutes and left at 0801". I was stunned.

It was just after 0803 hrs.

The cabbie had come and gone, and I wasn't there on time.

I've never forgotten the lesson the lady driver taught me that morning.

One evening the Seminar authorities put on a Chamber Concert for the Fellows.

Candlelight danced a sublime duet with the live orchestra. Mozart in the air, music for the soul!

One afternoon a few of us decided to go out into Salzburg proper. We walked around, savouring the sights and enjoying the cafes.

We clambered aboard a local bus to make it back to the Schloss for dinner.

I was sitting in the front of the bus.

From behind me I heard a commotion. I turned around.

Saw a furious elderly Austrian matron.

Her face was red, shaking her fists, shouting. At first, I couldn't fathom why.

And then the shocking truth dawned.

She'd seen and recognised the name badges that a couple of my friends had worn.

Israelis, Jewish.

I could make out the word "Juden" that she kept screaming. Horrifying!

Memories of Matthausen and Auschwitz. In this day and age!

Though I was shaken, my Israeli friends were not. "This is to be expected. Reminds us to never forget".

Haunting words!

They remind me every day that hate permeates the world. Are love and compassion fighting a losing battle?

War, torture, famine, climate change, an endless list of suffering. Brought on by greed, ego and selfishness.

But hope springs eternal.

Maybe the soul stirring music of Mozart could unite us all.

And maybe, just maybe, we could internalise the immortal prayer of St Francis of Assisi.

Lord, make me an instrument of thy peace. Amen.

16. Thunderbird Tales

As I stepped out of the aircraft the heat hit me. Blast from a furnace.

110F/43.3C at 2100 hrs!

Gosh, if this is the temperature so late in the evening, God help me in daytime!

12 August 1981.

My cherished dream of studying in the US was unfolding. I'd arrived in Phoenix, Arizona.

Enrolled at the American Graduate School of International Management located (then) in Glendale, Arizona.

The school was famous for its Master of International Management program.

It was informally known as Thunderbird after Thunderbird Airfield which was used to train pilots during World War 2.

Thunderbird is also a mythical creature revered by native American tribes[18], for its strength and potential to create transformation.

---

[18] *Revered by the Lakota (Sioux), Ojibwe (Chippewa), Ho-Chunk (Winnebago), Menominee, Algonquin, Kwakwaka'wakw (Kwakiutl) and Zuni tribes*

As a Rotary Ambassadorial Scholar, I would spend the next year immersed in the intricacies of global economics, finance and management.

Rotarian Bob Sexton, my designated local guardian, was at the airport with his charming wife Evelyn.

Caring and considerate to the extreme, Bob and Evelyn opened their home and hearts to me.

I stayed with them for a week, until I found a shared apartment just off campus.

Rushing every morning at 0755 hrs to be in class at 0815 hrs.

I'd have to be extremely careful running across the field to get into class. Because the field was infested with black widow spiders.

A bite would be an extremely painful baptism!

Dr McMahon had been very clear: either be in the classroom before 0815 hrs or don't bother coming.

I walked into that first class full of excitement, 0805 hrs. The room was full.

I was the only Indian. Curious glances.

I could almost hear them think. What's this guy doing here?

A female student was sitting in the first row.

Wearing a negligible pair of shorts, wide above the knees almost like a skirt.

Her legs were perched on the faculty desk. I sat next to her.

The door opened at 0814 hrs and Dr McMahon barreled in.

I shot to my feet out of conditioning.

You had to stand when the teacher arrives when I grew up in India. To my utter chagrin, no one else stood.

Sheepishly, I looked around, felt looks getting curiouser and sat down. The girl next to me continued chewing gum, her feet still on the desk. So much for respecting teachers!

Teachers, oh what an awesome lot!

Dr. Heathcotte who hardwired into memory …concepts like present value of money.

Dr Foster who taught me that an open book exam is much tougher than a traditional test.

Whose grading commenced at 100% and then he'd take off points for mistakes.

Dr Kim, the inscrutable Korean expert on International Banking. Who'd give us a simple reading assignment for the next class.

500 pages of arcane, esoteric, and empirical banking and finance concepts and case studies.

If you'd not read the material, forget it. Don't attend the class and don't expect to get a grade either.

The discipline of studying for 18 hours straight was like Samurai training. It came in handy 20 years later when I served on the Board of a bank[19].

And then, Dr. McMahon who encouraged me so much by taking me on as his Teaching Assistant.

---

[19] *See Imposter! in this book*

He'd ask me to grade the tests and assignments of students taking 300 level courses (lower than the 400 & 500 levels).

His approach to deadlines and work submissions laid the foundation for my thinking much later on the concept of Resultocracy[20].

He had a simple but devastatingly effective method.

Say, your assignment is due at 1700 hrs on a particular date. He'd set up a largish locked box with a slit outside his office. Like a ballot box.

Exactly at 1700 hrs on the appointed date he would open the box. If your assignment was in the box he'd grade it.

If it wasn't, well then, tough luck. You'd get a big fat F for FAIL.

That's it, no explanation, no discussion, no nothing.

Imagine the effectiveness of compliance and all the attendant learning! Classic use of Catalytic Mechanisms of which I've been a lifelong votary. The student body was truly global.

I made lifelong friendships with people from around the world. Karen who taught me the ropes around the campus.

Bob who was inspirational as President of the student body.

Mark who suddenly collapsed in the seat next to me during International Finance & Trade (IFT) class.

And in the process showed me the effectiveness of 911.

Within 5 minutes a helicopter landed almost next to the class room to administer to Mark.

---

[20] *Concept explained in my book Lonely At The Top: Reflections of A Mentor*

Christine's sweet French/British accent was endearing, even when she stayed with us in Kochi some 30 years later with her entire family.

Doug, God bless his soul[21], impressed me with his intellect and two Master's degrees.

Ricky the Texan wunderkind who took me to his home in Brownsville for Christmas.

That was the December 1981

Threatened by the Solidarity movement born in the Lenin Shipyard, Gdansk, the Communist Party in Poland felt impelled to act.

General Wojchiech Jaruzelski was tasked to take power and quash Solidarity.

Wearing his trademark dark glasses, he became a sinister presence on the global stage.

That power grab in Poland was one of the acorns out of which grew a mighty oak that upended the invincible Soviet empire.

The situation in Poland was much discussed in Brownsville that day. Ricky's entire family got busy cooking Christmas lunch.

His job was to make dessert.

Being the fabulous pastry chef that he is, Ricky put salt instead of sugar into the custard.

The family let out a loud, collective "Yuckkkk" after tasting it.

Since he'd laboured over making the custard for hours, I ate it without wincing.

---

[21] *Doug passed away in 2019*

We still laugh about it!

Thunderbird was just so much fun, quite apart from the backbreaking academic load.

So many characters, good friends all! And such great times!

Marie the Frenchwoman chased me around the cafeteria because I'd slipped ice cubes down the back of her blouse.

Nalini, who couldn't figure out who kept banging on her door and disappearing at 2 am (no prizes for guessing who that was).

Pascal, a fellow Rotary Scholar, the busybody Frenchman.

Dieter from Netherlands against whom I was locked in battle for 2 hours on the tennis court.

In 42 C heat, the court surface was hotter.

So hot that both of us could hardly walk after the match with blisters the size of marbles on our feet.

Mans the intellectual Swede.

Paul, the Dutch joker in our Marketing project group.

Andy, the affable American who was once stuck in a Russian toilet without toilet paper and had to use some old newspaper.

Almost creating an international incident by labelling the Taiwanese team as China instead of the Republic of China while they sat next to the team from People's Republic of China.

That was at Thunderbrains Quiz Competition that I'd launched at the school.

Good, solid, Dave, my roommate in East Apartments (on campus during the second semester) with whom I'd talk deeply about life and economics late into the night.

And, Matt, of course!

Born in South Africa, brought up in Malaysia, Indonesia and the Netherlands.

Lived and worked in the US and all over the world. Then came to Thunderbird.

My roommate for the final semester. Embodiment of time management and planning.

The lasting image in my mind is a relaxed Matt lounging in an armchair during Finals Week.

He'd not touched his books at all during this fateful, high-pressure week. Because he'd planned and worked so diligently, well in advance.

So, well that he'd pocket a 4.0 GPA!!

Rumour has it that Matt was pondering his next course of action even when he was just a twinkle in Dad's eye.

Some 42 years later we're still close! As I am with so many others.

I learnt so many life-altering lessons on that campus, in that space-time. Not just an education or an academic program…

Thunderbird was certainly one of the best years of my life.

It spun a magical mystique[22] and enriched me with tales to tell for a lifetime.

---

[22] *Thunderbird Mystique is still talked about as a non-definable quality that it imbues in its graduates*

17. Maha…Raja

I first saw him in 1999 at a meeting in Vapi, Gujarat, India.

"Meet Professor Raja. He's going to help us build this business school". That was the visionary Rotary leader Kalyan Banerjee[23] introducing us.

The dignified elderly gentleman was sitting quietly in a corner, as his wont. As I drew close, he got up.

Prof KCR Raja.

"Pleased to meet you," he said with a shy smile and extended his hand.

A hand of friendship, kinship and encouragement, extending over 25 years. A relationship quite unlike any other in my life.

Absolute trust and total respect.

Prof Raja was and will always be the epitome of everything that is good and great in a human being.

Undoubtedly one of the doyens, indeed, a father, of management education in India.

Author of many, many books including one on Ethics. And myriads of articles and case studies.

Teacher and mentor and Guru to thousands upon thousands of professional managers.

---

[23] *Kalyan went on to become the 3rd Indian to become President of Rotary International…in 2011-12*

Many of whom have risen to positions of power and influence in organizations around the world.

It's been a unique privilege working and conducting countless meetings and academic sessions alongside him.

A ringside view of how a true Master lives and works. Soft spoken to the extreme.

Not even the semblance of a harsh word escapes his lips.

That's because his entire being is as radiant as the sun which prevents darkness at source.

Affection, courtesy, and dignity personified. Nothing loud or brash.

Self-effacing to the core.

Substance, the deepest knowledge spanning the entire spectrum.

Economics, management, social sciences, art, history, music, dance, literature (English and Malayalam).

You name it. His is the last word you can count on it! His views are crystal clear.

Articulated in the gentlest of ways.

Each word dripping with meaning and significance.

Analysis that makes you think in dimensions that were invisible.

A 15-minute discussion with him is more enriching than a lifetime of classroom study.

Dedication that is almost indescribable.

Once, we had to travel to Vapi for an important meeting at the business school.

I could tell that he wasn't too well.

"I've had a minor surgical procedure so I'll need to be careful. If so, why don't you skip the meeting or I'll request them to postpone it. No, no. That will cause a lot of inconvenience to everyone who's attending. I'll be ok, don't worry."

Next morning I arrived at 0630 hrs to pick him up from his residence in Mumbai.

We had a four- and half-hour drive ahead of us to Vapi.

As he got into the car, I noticed that he was holding on to something inside his right trouser leg.

I was concerned. "What is it?"

"Why are you straightening the leg so gingerly? Oh, it's nothing just a urine bag".

I couldn't believe what I'd just heard.

Prof Raja had a catheter attached to a urine bag.

And he was travelling in the car to Vapi for a meeting, nearly 200 km away!

Throughout the journey we were discussing various ideas and solutions.

When we took a break at Annam Restaurant midway to Vapi, he was right behind me.

To savour hot idlis drowned in sambar.

Not once did he mention, let alone complain about, pain or discomfort.

Every intervention he made, every word, every thought and idea, they were all priceless treasures.

Watching and learning in his shadow I could feel the change in myself. I became much calmer and more considered in my approach to life.

What stands out most is his commitment to learning. Prof Raja is learning every moment!

I arrived in Kozhikode on 19 June 2022 to speak at his 90th birthday celebration.

The first thing he said to me was awe inspiring. "I'm doing a course on digital marketing." Learning, irrespective of age or circumstance.

There's no good or bad experience only a learning experience. He's a walking, talking example of that.

And he wears the crown quite literally, very hesitantly, Reluctantly, almost entirely embarrassed.

Because he is the Second in Line to the throne[24] Zamorin of Malabar.

Samoothiri in Malayalam, derived from the Sanskrit Samudri meaning the "Lord of The Sea".

Hereditary rulers of Kozhikode (Calicut) in the Malabar region of Kerala. With a proud history of resisting colonial rule.

Custodians of art, literature, kathakali indeed, all culture.

---

[24] *At this point of writing, 17 December 2024*

Trustees of the all-important Guruvayur Temple and many others (including Peringottukavu Bhagavathy Temple and Mammiyoor Temple).

Nobility and royalty flows in Prof Raja's veins.

The joke between us has always been the possibility of a formal coronation. But formal or not, he's a King in every respect.

Humility, self-improvement, selfless service and intellectual depth make him a titan of our times.

A true Maha... Raja.

18. Egobusting!

As a 16-year-old I was insufferable on the tennis court.

Playing a brand of copybook, aggressive tennis only Achan[25] could have taught me!

The pain I felt in my feet and ankles was channelled into a burning hunger to win by intense training under his watchful eyes[26].

The result was zero tolerance for errors from my doubles partners or indeed, anyone I was practising with.

If my partner missed a point or made a mistake, I would scream at him in full public view, even during a match.

I was so far ahead of anyone else, no one could match my perfection or so I thought.

Once, during a match and tournament that my partner Pankaj and I won, I crossed all lines of obnoxious behaviour.

---

[25] *Achan, my revered father, had been a renowned tennis player and sportsman in Travancore; he was Travancore State No.1 and hundreds of spectators used to throng his matches, enjoying the most stylish picture-perfect brand of attacking tennis that he played he was my tennis coach and.... Guru!*
[26] *I suffered from a condition called Navicular Accessories which resulted in swollen feet. I had to give up tennis for 2 years between the ages of 14 and 16; when I returned to the court at age 16 I had to wear special orthopaedic shoes with heavy steel supports embedded in then; this sometimes caused my ankles to twist, resulting in unbearable pain...*

Throughout the matches, in every game, on almost every point, I was literally yelling at Pankaj.

He just couldn't do anything without hearing from me! I was throwing tantrums and my racket, left right and centre. Pankaj just couldn't take it anymore.

After winning the doubles final with him I was riding back home on my bicycle.

Just as I was turning into my lane, a Vespa scooter swerved around me and stopped right in front of my bike.

It was Pankaj.

And he had a big tough guy riding pillion. I alighted and looked at them.

Got my racket ready, just in case.

Pankaj let fly with the choicest abuse in Hindi.

His friend growled at me, something to the effect that if I raised my voice by so much as half an octave against

Pankaj, ever again, he'd come back with 10 others and kill me!

Fortunately, there was no violence that day. But I had pushed Pankaj beyond limits.

A couple of weeks later the unthinkable happened when Pankaj was riding his scooter.

The handlebar of the scooter turned left and locked suddenly. while being driven at speed.

Pankaj shot over the handlebar, he passed away on the spot, all of 16 years of age.

I can still feel the agony, remorse, and sorrow.

That tragedy gouged out a deep wound inside me, a wound that's still not healed fully.

I began to calm down on the court.

But the old demons came out to play now and then.

In those days Achan would sometimes hold free tennis coaching clinics for youngsters.

All of whom would barely get two points in a set with me.

One afternoon, he gathered all of them, some 20 of them and got me to hit a few balls with another player.

As a kind of demonstration.

Of what I'd find out soon enough.

Some 5 minutes into the session I began to feel a sinking sensation in the pit of my stomach.

"Your elbow is sticking out ahead of your wrist on the forehand, that's why you're hitting the ball too high and out of the court".

The right foot is not across and pointing 45 degrees for your backhand.

Why's your left shoulder not aligned with the net for your forehand down the line?

Your service ball toss is too short.

What's wrong with your footwork and speed of movement? And you're not watching the ball properly."

All this in a stern tone of voice, a tone I'd hardly ever heard from Achan. For all the other kids to hear.

Some of them were tittering in glee.

I was being taken to the cleaners and they were enjoying it hugely.

Payback for all the humiliation I'd heaped on them on the court whenever we played.

Right there, in front of every player I was routinely thrashing in every game, Achan punctured my ego and brought me crashing down to earth.

He had decided that I needed a strong lesson…and not just in tennis. I was so crushed I could barely stand on the court.

Achan quietly picked up his racket and walked off. I followed him an hour later.

Not a word was spoken about any of this when I got home.

He had taught me to be more grounded and less full of myself.

Not to let arrogance soar into the stratosphere just because I was playing decent tennis.

My behaviour on court and off it improved significantly.

And, a few years later, I had the sublime experience of playing with Achan. Father and son doubles team!

In an open tournament.

The drill was that Achan would control the baseline.

I would dart to the net and kill any ball that rose more than 6 inches above the tape.

His fast, kicking serve would elicit a weak return and there I was at the net to put away a volley.

We won several matches until we lost to a fancied team in the semifinals. He was over 60 at the time!

And yet we made it to the semis…only because of his presence alongside me.

Achan always encouraged me when we played as a team. Never showed the slightest irritation or anger if I missed a shot. My manners changed completely on the tennis court after that.

I began to grin and bear it when mistakes were made by me or my partners.

And made stronger, lifelong friendships in the bargain.

All because Achan had spotted my trajectory and decided to nip it in the bud.

Right there, in front of all those kids on that hot afternoon in Ahmedabad, the demons had been driven away.

Not a tennis lesson…just, pure ego busting!

19. Loyalty...

Larene joined me in 1984.

When all I had was a dream, an idea and empty pockets! I had a small office.

But I knew that a Secretary was the best investment I could make. Furniture and fittings don't maketh a business.

People, their commitment and creativity do! I wanted the best.

So, I released an ad.

Wanted: creative, smart and result orient people who can work with me to build the dream.

Lots of people applied.

Secretaries with years of experience. I fielded many phone calls.

What's the job?

How big is the company?

Salary, working hours, type of industry...the questions were all justified.

And my answer was: I really don't know; we've got to create something new.

That was enough to scare off most of the applicants.

When they found out that candidates would have to take a dictation test, followed by a Test of Reasoning and

Current Affairs and finally, an interview. Well, that was the straw which broke the camel's back.

The rest of them disappeared, except Larene.

A smartly turned lady with short hair and a ready smile. A look of surprise overtook her face.

She'd expected a middle-aged man. And there I was, the MD, all of 29!

With some far-out ideas that she couldn't understand!

There was no one else and no furniture except my desk and chair…and an old typewriter on a ramshackle table in the other room.

Nervousness and uncertainty overtook her.

I tried to reassure her with mention of writing and dictation and how interesting and fun the test would be.

That did it.

She was a wreck by the time I produced the test. The first few questions were pretty routine.

And then I'd slipped in some reasoning puzzles. "Coffee has caffeine."

Caffeine is a drug.

Therefore, coffee is a drug. True or False?

Larene stumbled through the test. But her typing was superb.

Everything about her was professional, honest and straightforward. The test result be damned.

From her behaviour and speech, I could tell she was a real gem.

Right there I offered her the job and she accepted the very next day.

A lady with years of experience in big companies joins me who had nothing.

She'd earned my total respect.

Over the next year she did something I can never forget. Something for which I'm eternally grateful.

My ideas were great, but where was the money? First generation entrepreneur with no cash.

We had to pay for our first set of computers or lose it all. We needed Rs 50,000/- desperately within a week.

I had no idea where to get it from. Every source had dried up.

Desperation escalated into near panic.

That's when Larene walked in and placed a plastic bag on my table. "Here's Rs 50,000/-[27]. Please take it. I know you'll do the right thing." I was dumbfounded.

"How'd you get this? My husband's property was sold a few days ago and this is part of the proceeds. He's given this to me for safekeeping. It was in my cupboard. Did you tell him that you're giving it to me? No. No one knows."

Here was this lady, who'd been working with me for just a few months, trusting me with the money, her marriage, her family, her life

Flabbergasted!

Unbelievable and incredible. This was the honour of my life.

---

[27] *Approximately Rs 7,50,000/- today at an interest rate of 7 % per annum*

When someone puts this level of trust in you what do you do? Well, you try desperately to be worthy of that trust!

I begged, borrowed, did not steal, and scrounged enough somehow to quickly replace the money in her cupboard. And no one ever knew.

Today, a full four decades later, she's still a highly respected member of my family.

Larene is a devout Catholic.

With that one act of total trust and unconditional faith she taught me the true meaning of Catholicism and loyalty.

Unwavering.

Under all conditions. No ifs and buts.

Total.

That's loyalty…

20. Overwrite!

1400 hrs on a Friday afternoon in 1994. I was rushing to meet a deadline.

A 10,000-word booklet entitled, "How To Manage Your Money" for The Week, India's No.1 weekly magazine in terms of circulation.

I'd been slaving over it for several days.

Writing and explaining concepts like the Present Value of Money, Risk Return Principle and so on.

In between my responsibilities, running our computer education institute.

We'd named it Expert Information Technology P Ltd. when it was set up in 1987.

I'd read a book then on Expert Systems and knew in my bones that this was the future.

A future captivated by AI.

So, my writing was in fits and starts over many days. Punctuated with all kinds of operational challenges.

But it was already Friday and I had to submit my final manuscript by 1700 hrs.

Only then could the magazine produce the booklet to be distributed with their latest edition hitting the stands on Monday.

I'd spent countless hours tapping out asdf..lkj on Typing Tutor.

After months of dreary practice, I was reasonably comfortable typing on my PC.

Though I was nowhere near Mary's speed on the keyboard. She'd joined me just a few days earlier as Secretary.

She was a trained typist and had worked for many years as Secretary to the MD of a large company.

Word processing and computers were new to her and to almost everyone.

By then, Larene had transitioned mostly to administrative work. She was showing Mary the ropes.

"Your boss is a tough nut to crack".

She'd already given Mary a heads up on what to expect!

Understandably, the newbie was a little apprehensive about the new environment…

And me.

What kind of a colleague, boss would I be? At 1400 hrs I was done with the booklet.

"Mary, can you and Larene please take this file, do a proof check and format it properly so that we can send it off to The Week?"

Soon, Mary and Larene got busy, peering into the screen and correcting the typos.

After about 90 minutes I heard a gasp.

Loud enough for me to hear in the other room.

I knew instinctively that something nasty had transpired. I rushed out.

"What happened?"

Mary and Larene were speechless.

From their blanched faces I had an inkling. "Doesn't matter, tell me what's the problem?" I was trying to stay as cool as possible.

"We've lost the entire document you gave us to proof read..and we can't find a backup on the computer."

Larene was in tears and so was Mary. "You mean all 10,000 words are lost? "Yes, the entire document is wiped out. How?"

We'd just finished proof corrections and formatting and were trying to save. A message popped up on screen:

Do you want to Overwrite? Y or N

We pressed Y by mistake. The entire file was gone.

Deleted.

Without a trace.

No backups.

Both of them were waiting for me to explode.

But my mind was racing. It was 1530 hrs.

90 minutes more to the deadline. We weren't going to make it.

So, I called the Editor[28], a dear friend of mine.

"Gopal, I have a problem. I've lost the entire file containing the booklet. Can you please give me some more time to re-do it?"

---

[28] *TR Gopalakrishnan, a legendary journalist who'd played a pivotal role in the success of The Week*

He was sympathetic and understanding.

"Can you get it to me by 1700 hrs on Sunday?"

"Yes. I'll make sure that you get it, this time there'll be no glitches". I didn't know how in God's name I would meet this deadline.

Well, I've got to try.

There wasn't any point at all in shouting at Mary and Larene. They're already feeling miserable about the entire snafu.

Guilty that they'd failed me. That was suffering enough.

I couldn't add chillies to a raw wound.

"Ok, guys, let's learn from this. Never press a key again unless you're sure about what it's going to do. Let's get on with it."

I went back into my cave. And recreated the manuscript, word by word from memory.

As and when I'd typed a couple of paras, I'd get Mary to copy it and work on proof checking and formatting with Larene.

Both of them stayed overnight in the office.

Despite familial responsibilities…and societal outrage. Friday night, all night we worked, the three of us.

Time stopped.

Come Saturday morning, we were still labouring over it. And Saturday night and Sunday afternoon.

Nonstop with no breaks except for hurried meals ordered in. Both of them devoted themselves to the cause.

I've never ever experienced this kind of dedication. before or after, Day and night we slogged and delivered. By Sunday 1700 hrs, the manuscript was with The Week. Mission accomplished.

Mary and Larene had rebounded from the mistake!

With grit and determination, they'd not only overcome the problem but learnt from it.

I was so very proud of them!

It was a huge learning experience for me too.

One that has shaped my thinking on leadership and results.

Mistakes are not opportunities to punish, rather they're opportunities for improvement.

Debrief, not destroy!

Today, 30 years later, Mary still supports me, minute to minute.

Perhaps my behaviour that day had something to do with it, perhaps. But in any case, she's earned my undying gratitude.

By staying the course, and overcoming Overwrite!

21. Death Threat!

The envelope was innocuous. Not the contents.

"A bomb is going to blow you to bits along with your computer training institute."

No one knew how it arrived on the reception desk.

It seemed that we'd become a real threat to the competition. Others were struggling to keep their heads above water.

But we were flush with students.

More than 500 youngsters were learning the intricacies of programming in our facilities.

Many would go on to become leaders of India's emergence as an IT superpower.

Problem solving approaches, system design, programming in various languages, tests, projects, presentations.

It was a beehive of activity.

Bright minds being honed to razor sharpness on the cutting-edge of technology.

There wasn't any bandwidth for laxity or unprofessional behaviour. Word of mouth ensured a continuous number of enrolments.

No wonder the competition was jittery. So, the threat was real. Danger lurked.

When I read the note, it was clear that it was mostly aimed at me personally. This wasn't new to me.

Once, at a conference in Delhi I'd raised strong objections to arbitrary policies.

After the conference I was followed by a couple of tough looking men. When I stopped, turned and faced them they just melted away.

The note spurred me into action.

Got the security and staff to be alert and look for unusual activity. Eliminate loitering. Check ids carefully, observe strangers.

I spoke to the Police Commissioner.

He was kind enough to post plainclothes cops in our Front Office for a week.

I sent the note to Police HQ; they tried to lift fingerprints from the paper. To no avail; there were far too many smudges and no clear prints.

The next morning Nandan came to see me quietly. During his inspection he'd spotted a serious problem. A light bulb was found removed.

And a 25 paise coin was twisted into the light socket.

The idea was at the very least to cause a calamitous short circuit. And a devastating fire at worst.

In an environment full of people and electronic equipment.

Diabolic.

A follow up to the threat note.

Of course, we took every step necessary to secure the premises. The plainclothes policemen followed a possible suspect.

We obtained some clues; but nothing substantive. Obviously, we were being watched.

So, our alertness sent a strong message.

We were not about to be rolled over without a fight! Nothing untoward happened thereafter.

But we were constantly on edge.

Keeping an eye out for suspicious objects or people. The threat had been real.

But I felt vindicated.

We were making an impact. Strong enough to make waves.

And fuel insecurities large enough to create a threat.

The experience of being physically targeted taught me a great lesson.

An individual or organisation that is clear about values and is committed to them presents a very uncomfortable situation for others.

Mediocrity is comfortable.

But chasing excellence is by definition difficult and unpopular among peers.

So, the path is lonely and oftentimes unlit. Dark shadows can hold dangers at every turn. You have to be your own light!

I dedicated myself to building self-sufficiency and internal strength. And so, in a way, I was thankful.

To the threat!

22. MBA

"**I**'ve just got admission into the MBA Program of School of Management Studies (SMS) of Cochin University.[29]"

MBA? What's that?

MBA was a novelty in India in the mid-1970s. Hardly anyone had heard of it.

And yet, India was home to some great institutions imparting management education.

School of Management Studies in Cochin, SMS was one of them arguably among the best.

Set up by the visionary educationist and ultimate expert on the Constitution of India, Dr M.V. Pylee (founding Director of SMS and later, Vice Chancellor of Cochin University)

SMS, in keeping with Dr Pylee's world class standards, was choosy about its students.

The selection process was actually a rigorous, test and interview-based elimination process.

In August 1976, some 30 odd eager beaver would-be managers filed into the classroom.

The legendary Dr Pylee walked in with his trademark stoop. Without much ado he welcomed us and then dropped the bomb.

---

[29] *Cochin University of Science & Technology (CUSAT) as it is known now.*

"This program is unlike anything you've previously experienced. Don't think you can cram just before the exam and pass. You'll have to work hard every minute. Because you'll be under severe academic pressure. Your evaluation will be continuous."

Many of us thought we could wing it like we'd done before. I knew nothing else.

My motto throughout my career as a student hitherto was, "study only if its unavoidable!"

I was in for a rude shock, as were my classmates.

Reading assignments, case studies, tests, presentations, group work, piled on till we were brought to the brink of collapse.

Signs of incipient rebellion began to be visible.

Nipped in the bud by the faculty with more course work. No time or ability to gossip or organise.

Study or fail.

It was a stark choice.

So, we buckled down and worked.

During that first month I was elected Class Representative. The shortest of honeymoons followed.

Within a few weeks, my classmates wrote a letter of "No Confidence In Madhav Mohan," to the Director.

I was flung out unceremoniously!

In way that was good because I could then focus on what I'd never done, study and work consistently. Since we were on a 24-hour clock, Friday night was like an oasis in the desert.

Our hostel rooftop was converted into a raucous party venue. Liquor, all kinds, was poured into a big bucket.

Rum, whiskey, beer, you name it and it was all mixed in. Plastic mugs doubled as cups.

At first my batchmates would ask me to join.

Then they'd cajole, threaten, and finally deride me as a lost cause because I wouldn't join!

Sometimes we'd chuck all the work and scoot off for a "second show" at a movie theatre 2 kms away.

The "second show" was a show which commenced at 9:30 pm and generally stretched until midnight.

Hindi and Malayalam movies were interminably long!

Walking back to the hostel at midnight was quite the experience. Everyone was clad in lungis and shirts.

A bunch of unlikely managers belting out popular songs tunelessly in the dead of night.

Ajay(an) was undoubtedly the star in our class.

Humorous and irreverent to the core.

He was the go-to person for entertainment and on demand composition of lyrics, ditties and songs!

The night walk wasn't complete without Ajayan's wisecracks and jokes.

Once, we'd deliberately ditched the Accounting assignment and made off for the second show!

As we came up the hill and around the bend, SMS came into view. It was 12:30 am.

The Faculty Room on the second floor was ablaze with lights. And in the window, we espied KKG (our Accounting Professor).

He knew that we'd dumped his assignment and was waiting to identify the errant.

So that he could score us appropriately in the class next morning. Ajayan gave us the command, one, two…

On the count of three, all lungis were lifted and tied over the head. By everyone.

The hapless KKG could only see mass underwear.

All faces and heads were covered by the respective lungi!!

And then Ajayan spontaneously burst into song with the chorus chiming in.

Something to the effect in colourful Malayalam that the root cause of all difficulties was KKG.

Loud enough for him to hear, Faceless underwear mocking him! But who was he going to penalise? He couldn't identify anyone.

Next morning, every one of us got a big fat FAIL grade.

But the fun we had to earn this lifelong memory was worth the grade and then some!

Coming out of Loyola College, Madras (now Chennai) with a Gold Medal in the MA Economics program, my pride and ego knew no bounds.

And it reflected in all my interactions during the First Semester of the MBA program.

Prof Lukose, meanwhile, had attained cult status in the academic and student community.

Barrel chested and taciturn.

Scowling with a pipe dangling jauntily from his lips.

Expert in behavioural science and military in bearing and background.

He'd given us the MMPI[30] assessment test and compiled dossiers on every one of us.

Personality vagaries of each student lay bare in his hands. Passionate about helping each one attain his potential.

Strict disciplinarian, but caring to the core.

He was convinced that I was the ideal candidate for Sensitivity Training. He couldn't have been more right and bless him for his insight!

One morning I was asked to report to the classroom at 0930 hrs.

I walked in and found my entire class sitting around the horseshoe table.

"Madhav, please take the seat at the head of the table," Prof Lukose's gravelly voice commanded.

I sat down and he sat in a chair behind and to my right.

Eager anticipation was writ large on the faces of my classmates. This was their chance to get even with me.

Abuse.

Four letter word.

---

[30] *Minnesota Multiphase Personality Inventory..a widely used psychological tool used to assess personality structure..originally developed in the 1930s.*

Detailed recounting, every bit of my past behaviour was read back to me. In the most unflattering and crude manner.

Everything was thrown at me. No holds barred.

For 5 full hours I was subjected to verbal third degree treatment. Forced to listen.

Face the music, fully, frontally.

I wasn't allowed to say anything, couldn't open my mouth.

After a while the session became so painful that I developed a stress headache.

I couldn't look anyone in the eye.

Mercifully, Prof Lukose handed me a pair of sunglasses. He was taking copious notes.

For days after that session, I was in a daze. I literally didn't know what had hit me.

And then I began to think, "Maybe I'm not God, after all. All these guys can't be wrong."

I had to introspect and change and I did, for the better.

In that classroom, in the middle of that trauma, Prof Lukose had set me on the path to personal growth.

Through it all he guided me gently but firmly. I'm eternally grateful to him.

In later years we became close friends.

And I became a better person, hopefully, after the Sensitivity Training. Like every batch we thought we were special!

But my classmates were indeed extraordinarily talented and smart.

All of them went on to become spectacularly successful businessmen and professionals around the world.

My Bad Attitude had been transformed into an MBA.

23. Marks & Tennis

The BA (Economics) final year results were out. And they were horrendous for me.

I'd barely scraped through with an ignominious third class.

The unkindest cut of all was the English language score: in the low thirties! Achan[31] bore the brunt of it.

"Nair Sir, I'm so sorry to hear of your son's poor showing. Mali Sir, how did he get such a low score?"

"Malichetta, you're such a colossal literary figure; how did your son turn out this way"

These were all direct questions.

Behind his back the comments were more like "Mali's son is such a dumb creature.

What a waster!

How did that happen? And that too in such a great family". The answer was very clear, not rocket science.

I was simply too preoccupied to study!

Tennis had been my focus.

Training and playing tournaments in Gujarat and around the country.

---

[31] *My illustrious, revered father, V.Madhavan Nair "Mali"*

Hardly went to class because St Xavier's College and Gujarat University had been lenient about attendance since I was the University champion.

Bottom line: I simply did not make the effort to get a good score, let alone pass!

And so, at age 19, there I was a Third Class degree holder. With no prospects and a dim future.

Tennis wasn't going to get me anywhere, at least not in those days.

I was panic stricken. What do I do?

The first thing is to correct my marks. Which means doing an MA in Economics. But where?

With my poor BA marks who's going to give me admission for MA? Then I remembered.

Loyola College, Chennai, the famous college with one of the best MA Economics programs in India.

They were also renowned for the standard of tennis played there. Maybe, just maybe…

One fine morning in August 1974, I found myself in a daunting office.

Father Kuriakose, Principal, Loyola College, had agreed to give me 5 minutes.

"Yes, what do you want?" he asked in a stern voice.

"Sir…" and I choked.

"Go on. I don't have all day".

"Sir, I want admission to MA Economics at Loyola".

"Show me your marks," and I did.

Father Kuriakose convulsed in derisive laughter.

"With these pathetic marks you want to get into the MA Economics course? You must be crazy. Get out of my office, now!" Unceremoniously thrown out.

I was desperate. I had to get in, somehow.

Else I was looking at being a lower division clerk in some dreary office for the rest of my life.

After that initial blowout I kept hanging around the Principal's office.

Every time Father Kuriakose went in or out, he'd see me but pretend he didn't.

Finally, after about 3 weeks, he couldn't pretend any longer. "Why are you still here? Didn't I tell you there's no chance? "Father, please, please listen to me, I'm a tennis player".

His ears perked up.

"Oh, you play tennis? Show me your certificates." I handed over my tennis credentials.

"Ok, young man. Go and see the Father in charge of tennis, Father Louis Xavier."

I ran like a soul possessed to find the God of Loyola tennis. He was just waking up from his afternoon siesta.

"What is it?"

"Father, the Principal asked me to see you. I'm a tennis player and I want admission to MA Economics.

Is that so? Are you a good player? We'll find out. Go and see the Tennis Captain".

I tracked down the Tennis Captain. Ranjit Yesudasan.

Captain of the fabled Loyola College Tennis Team feared by every team in the country.

"Ok, Madhav report to Court No.1 tomorrow at 3.30 pm to play a match against a player in our team." Ranjit was non-committal but cordial.

Next afternoon I was at Court No. 1 at 3 pm with my two rackets, one of them cracked but held together by tightly wound cat gut.

Court No.1 had iconic status. Loyola had 10 tennis courts.

A player has to start on Court 10 and work his way up by challenging higher ranked opponents.

If you played on Court 10 and challenged a player on Court 9 and won, well, you got promoted to Court 9 and he got demoted to Court 10.

So, you had to work your way up to Court No. 1 the hard way. It was simple. but devilishly tough.

Naturally, Court No.1 was the home of the very best players and the Loyola Team.

It was a dream court.

A fence separated it from the other courts. Ball boys in attendance.

And, unheard of luxury, new balls provided every day!

At any given time, a small crowd would gape at the quality of tennis. I'd walked into the lion's den.

My future hung in the balance.

The College Team member ambled in nonchalantly at 3.30 pm.

I'd known him from earlier meetings in Trivandrum… and at tournaments. We hit a few balls to warm up.

And the match began in right earnest

For me it was do or die, life and death, survival. For him it was just another match.

So who do you think won, 6-4?

Next morning, Principal gave me the Letter of Admission to MA Economics, Loyola College.

I continued to play tennis and not study. Soon, MA Finals were looming.

And I was totally unprepared.

Study leave commenced and I arrived in Palakkad, my grandfather's mansion.

Achan and Amma lived there too. Sheer terror and panic set in.

I didn't want to write the exam.

Scared that another near-fail result would kill me. I wanted to drop out.

Amma wouldn't hear of it!

In her gentle, clear and firm way she encouraged me.

"You still have 60 days. You're smart! If you study seriously from now, you'll still do well."

That changed my mindset.

But sheer terror and panic drove me to study about 9 to 10 hours per day. For some 60 days.

I'd wake up around 0600 hrs.

Amma's steaming coffee would bring me alive.

I'd hit the books at 0630 hrs and keep going till 0830. Then, a shower and breakfast.

Resume at 0930.

At 1100 Amma would tip toe in with a large mug of Horlicks. Study till 1300 hrs and break for lunch.

Resume at 1400 hrs, tea and snacks at 1530 hrs. Amma made sure that I got enough fuel for my brain.

Books were put away at 1745 hrs.

I wasn't one for night studies.

In the evening I'd chat with Achan and Amma and get my mind off Economics.

Lights out at 2130 hrs.

The work was tough but the routine was comforting because of Amma's loving presence.

9 to 10 hours of intense, focused study per day for 60 days. I went back to Madras (Chennai) and wrote the exams.

Since Mathematical Economics was my elective, I used the math approach in all my other electives as well.

So my answers were peppered with equations and derivations. I used fewer answer sheets than my peers.

Using this approach was a big gamble!

Relieved and relaxed, the exams were done and dusted. Maybe I'll pass!

A few weeks later, the MA Economics results were announced.

I'd won the Gold Medal in Economics…and stood first in Loyola College!

Did the maths approach have anything to do with it? The very same "well-wishers" called Achan again. "We knew your son was brilliant!"

Through it all Achan was unmoved.

He'd stood like a rock and had supported me through and through.

When I bombed in the BA Economics exam he just said, "Do better next time".

But when my MA results came in, he was thrilled! And Amma?

Well, she'd held me together when I was going to pieces.

When my result was announced I could see her smile and say "I told you so".

My secret weapons, Amma and Achan had seen me through! But I realized that marks were fickle indicators.

"If marks are good, you're smart and if they're bad, you're dumb," is a dangerous analysis.

The same person can score very different marks at different points in time. I'd learnt that they are a function of effort.

What you put in is what you get out as simple as that. They don't reflect your intellect or potential.

Throughout my career, interviewing thousands of people, I never forgot that marks were just one datapoint amongst many.

24. Facing Off

The meeting of the Board of Directors was interrupted. By a loud banging on the door.

Clearly an unruly commotion was happening just outside the Board Room. Unheard of in the staid corridors of a hierarchy laden bank.

In fact, the 7th Floor, the MD's floor, on which the Board Room was located, was out of bounds for "lesser mortals"!

The interruption was unprecedented.

The Board's aide opened the door and went outside to investigate. He came back in a hurry and in a tizzy.

"It's the Officer's Association. They're launching an agitation and are threatening to boycott Annual Closing if their demands are not met".

Annual Closing is crucial to a bank's operations.

It's the finalisation of accounts for the year and a prelude to putting out the financial statements the bank's performance, for the year.

Much discussion ensued amongst the Directors.

I was convinced the problem, whatever the problem, could be solved by direct communication between the stakeholders.

"Let's meet the Association and understand the situation." The MD concurred with me.

We sent word to the Association that we'll meet them in the adjoining conference room.

I led the group of 3 Directors and the MD into the conference room. Clearly the atmosphere was confrontational.

Tension so thick you could cut it with a breadknife.

A couple of unflattering slogans were raised when we entered. We sat down and looked at the agitated officers.

I began the conversation.

"We know you are upset about a lot of things. How important you are to the Bank is proven by the fact that the Board paused its meeting and a committee of Directors has stepped out to meet you. This has never happened before."

My conciliatory but mildly tough tone took them by surprise. Grievances began to be aired.

I raised my hand.

"This is not the forum to air grievances. We are here to show you how important you are. Meet the authorities of the Bank in the proper manner and discuss your issues with them. Once their report is in, the Board will discuss and decide immediately on the right course of action. You cannot hold the Bank to ransom by threatening to boycott Annual Closing. But I can assure you on behalf of all the Directors that the Bank will consider your demands in a fair manner. Now, get back to work. IMMEDIATELY."

Everyone was stunned!

They were not expecting this approach at all.

Quietly they filed out of the room, all the agitating officers.

Soon, we got word that the agitation had been called off. The Officers were back at work.

Annual Closing happened smoothly.

I learnt that personal credibility and courage can indeed move mountains, even in bureaucratic environments.

This situation was not new to me.

Some years earlier I'd found myself in an even more dire situation. We had organised a Karate tournament.

Inevitably, there were injuries during the bouts…some of them serious.

One of the fighters suffered a broken rib which had then punctured his lung.

He'd been rushed to hospital…and he recovered after a few days.

After the tournament was over, I looked for an autorickshaw (auto 3-wheeler) to go home.

It was 1:30 am.

No autos were in sight.

A flash strike was being enforced by auto drivers. So, I started walking, home was about 6 km away. From behind me I heard an engine.

Turning around I saw the outline of a vehicle with just parking lights on. Coming in my direction.

I waved him down.

It was an auto, the driver was on the road, flouting the strike. "Can you drop me home? Yes, but it's very risky. If we are spotted by the striking drivers." Prophetic words!

A couple of kilometres later we were puttering along stealthily. Suddenly, we were jumped by a mob.

Auto drivers who were waiting for strike breakers!

Out of the shadows they darted out and blocked our way. The auto shuddered to a stop.

Grabbed the driver by the scruff of his neck and yanked him out. I could hear the hiss of air as they punctured the tires.

Then they began thrashing the driver for daring to ply his trade when a strike had been called.

I'd been sitting quietly in the back seat.

When I saw the hapless man being set about, I lost my temper. Bounding out of the auto I roared at them at the top of my voice.

On a dark street with no lights, at 2 am, in the middle of an angry mob.

"How dare you stop my auto. Shame on you for beating a defenseless man. He was only helping me. Now, you've punctured the tires and there's no way I can reach home. Find me another auto or else I'm not budging".

They stopped in their tracks.

Here was a lone stranger bristling with anger and righteous indignation. There were 20 of them and 1 of me!

Anything could've happened. But it didn't.

The leader of the gang came up to me and shook my hand. "Sorry, sir. We'll drop you home. And this man, we'll let him go." He instructed one of the guys to go bring another auto.

Good sense and fair play had prevailed.

I reached home safely that night and so did my auto driver. What tipped the scales?

How did the situation, so pregnant with danger, get defused so peacefully?

I'd like to think it was righteous indignation. Righteousness is a shield.

An impenetrable forcefield which is a manifestation of the Divine.

25. What Am I?

Hi, Madhav, do you take classes in Mumbai? No.

Are you a consultant? No.

Are you a speaker? No.

Are you working with an organisation? No.

Are you a Professor, a banker, a writer maybe? No.

What is it that you do, exactly?

I've spent a lifetime answering these questions, often unsatisfactorily!

Many of my closest friends and relatives still don't have any idea of what I've been doing over the last 30 years!

I've been doing all of the above, and yet, not any of them!

Let me share some stories that may point to an understanding! Manoj was Senior Manager and he was clearly troubled.

"Hi, Manoj. Is something bothering you?

"Yes, Sir. It's about my wife. She's not her usual self. Over the last 45 days she's been moody, irritable and just too touchy. Gets angry at the drop of a hat, flies off the handle, and throws things. She was never like this. It's so bad that I can't sleep. It's affecting my work badly. What should I do?"

A sudden insight flashed in my consciousness. "Manoj, is she pregnant?

"No, I don't think so."

"Are you sure?"

"No, I'm not sure."

"Ok, why don't you take her to the doctor and get a test?"

Two weeks later when I returned to the factory Manoj sought me out.

"Sir, you were right. The doctor confirmed that my wife is pregnant. It was a complete surprise for her and for me. The doctor explained that hormonal changes can affect behaviour and indeed cause mood swings. Now I know how to deal with the situation. Thank you, sir!"

Shyam was confused and deeply concerned.

Though he'd been married for nearly 5 years his wife hadn't conceived. I knew that his work environment wasn't exactly healthy.

So, I told him to share his worry with his doctor immediately and ask if there was a connection with his workplace.

The doctor ran tests and told him that his sperm count was low.

The problem was tracked down to the physical environment in which he worked.

It was damaging Shyam's ability to father children.

Putting family above his job, Shyam moved to another company. And went on to become the proud father of two children!

For many, many years I used to conduct what I call Concept Workshops. This was an original idea which I'd converted into a pedagogy.

My premise was, and is, that people who learn together stay together. Relationships strengthen between co-learners.

If relationships become strong, collaboration flows.

When that happens, productivity improves and so does profitability, and finally, profits.

So, the Concept Workshop is a platform which builds a fraternity of learners who ultimately contribute to profits.

Study material would be circulated in advance. Attending the Concept Workshop is voluntary.

But, having committed to attending, study of the material is mandatory. So, I'd walk into a room full of well-prepared managers.

And together we'd proceed to create an environment of informality, fun and laughter.

I'd police the guardrails mercilessly: no one was allowed to be judgmental, pull rank or monopolise the discussions.

The result was a 4-hour freewheeling session in which people encouraged each other to share and accept differing points of view.

Mostly the discussions would relate to the material; but often they'd spin off into many different areas.

Communication and collaboration outside the Concept Workshop improved dramatically.

Once I'd demonstrated a concept from Karate during a Concept Workshop.

After the session, Naveen, a senior finance professional in his late 40s came to me.

"Sir, you've opened a new vista of growth for me. I'm going to train Karate".

Five years later he called me with great news and sent me an inspirational photo.

Naveen, his wife and their two daughters (CA toppers both) had been awarded black belts in Karate!

On another occasion I'd chanted the Madhurashtakam[32] and explained it as a template for personal growth.

A decade later I received thank you notes from some of the participants in that session.

From the thousands of man-hours of Concept Workshops I've gleaned that people can learn and achieve anything if they are accepted, understood, empowered and encouraged.

This is an insight that has dawned on many, many leaders when they experienced the Concept Workshop firsthand.

By holding up a mirror to leaders I learnt, along with them, what works and what doesn't.

Interviewing candidates, by the thousands, taught me to listen and spot strengths and exaggerations.

---

[32] *Composed by the saint Sri Vallabhacharya (1470-1531 CE) during the 15th-16th Century; he was the founder of the Pushti Marg (Path of Grace) a sect dedicated to Lord Krishna. The hymn Madhurashtakam describes every facet and aspect of Lord Krishna as filled with sweetness.*

Helping organizations and their people, clarify values, vision and then build strategy in hundreds of man-hours of Vision Workshops lifted the veil of confusion and revealed a clear path forward for me and mine.

Creating systems that allowed companies to go from being cash strapped to cash rich showed me how simple ideas can make big impacts.

Holding hundreds of man-hours worth of feedback sessions enabled me to show top leaders the right way to inspire and motivate their teams.

Writing columns and speaking at myriad venues on a wide range of subjects ranging from spirituality, leadership, economic policy, management systems, geo-strategic affairs, sports, aviation and military matters helped me learn new ideas and communicate them to a wide audience.

Nothing is more satisfying or impactful than assisting people and organizations attain clarity of thought and action on their own present and future.

I've often pondered on the common elements that went into my approach and work.

A deep interest in people and the environment in which they live and work.

Understanding the power, tools and facets of leadership and their practical application.

Examining the applicability of solutions from one field to problems in another.

Looking for patterns in data, behaviour, problems, opportunities. An eclectic world view.

Over and above anything else, an ironclad belief in the power and potential of individuals.

So, what does all that make me? You tell me!

26. Power Of Chanting

"Madhav, we've planned a day out at sea for you tomorrow". That was my dear friend Richard.

He'd invited me to Keri Keri in New Zealand to address a Rotary District Conference.

I'd spoken about how Rotary in India, had mobilised to alleviate sufferings caused by the terrible Gujarat Earthquake[33].

Now that the Conference was over, Richard the Conference Chairman was relaxed.

At 0800 hrs next morning he picked me up and we drove to his friend's home in Auckland.

Ian and his girlfriend were waiting for us.

They'd already brought out the trailer holding a beautiful white boat. Quickly, they attached the trailer to the tow bar behind Ian's car.

All of us piled in and we were off.

Close to the mouth of the bay we launched from a boat ramp. In a jiffy we were in the water!

---

[33] *The quake registered 7.7 on the Richter scale and struck at 0846 hrs IST on 26 January 2001. Epicentre was near Bhuj, Kutch District, State of Gujarat, India.*

Ian started the powerful motors and we made way towards the mouth of the bay.

Along the way, Ian and his girlfriend strung out a line behind the boat.

Just as we cleared the bay they pulled in the line. On the hooks were two large sturgeons.

That was my first shock!

They unhooked the live sturgeons.

And proceeded to disembowel the fish!

With a couple of deft swishes from his evil looking knife Ian cut open the first one.

He scooped his hand into the gaping hole and pulled out the innards and threw them into a bucket.

The fish was still convulsing, a mass of blood and gore.

Then he did the same to the second fish.

This time his hand was filled with a slimy white mass. Eggs! Millions of them!

Tossed into the bucket.

The sheer violence of it shook me to my core.

I'm a vegetarian and abhor violence against animals.

My belief systems were clearly, completely at odds with those of my hosts!

They were honouring me by taking the time, effort, and money to give me an experience of their way of life amidst the beauty of the sea.

I wished there was something I could say to make them understand my pain.

There was nothing I could do except to manage myself to avoid disrespecting them.

The sturgeons were only a sneak preview of what was to come.

Both the hapless fish were chopped into small pieces as bait and fastened to hooks.

These hooks were fixed at intervals to a line that ran some 500 metres behind the boat.

By the time we were fully out to sea the lines were in place. And then the killing began, on an industrial scale.

The line was pulled in little by little, 5 feet by 5 feet.

5 unlucky fish which had taken the bait and got hooked were freed. Only to be flung to the cutting board.

And disemboweled.

Slash, cut, grab entrails, throw entrails into bucket, throw the rest of the fish into ice box.

Sickening sound of steel on flesh. Spurt of blood.

Slosh of gore.

Nauseating smell of death.

The process repeated with metronomic precision. I counted some 60 fish, in lots of 5.

And I was standing right next to the killing.

There was no place else to be, it was a small boat.

After the first 15 minutes I thought I couldn't take it anymore. Then, suddenly I heard a whisper in my ear.

"Chant, Chant!"

And I started chanting.

"Hare Krishna Hare Krishna Krishna Krishna Hare Hare Hare Rama Hare Rama Rama Rama Hare Hare."

Quietly, under my breath. Over and over again.

Countless times, till we got back to shore. I couldn't change anyone or anything.

The Mahamantra was the buoy I clung to in the storm of violence. The sight, the smell, the sounds, all were deflected by the chant. A calm descended on the turbulence of my heart and mind.

I watched every little thing that was happening right under my nose.

No expression on my face, no nausea. completely present but not part of it.

Being there without being there.

The pain gave way to peace, a peace that I think also extended to the fish in their final suffering.

After all, their last moments were in the company of the Mahamantra. No one else could hear it, but they could feel the vibrations.

That was the best I could do.

Let them feel the Holy Name so that they could merge in it. I'd like to think that their release was painless.

For me, it was life altering.

Richard, bless him, had created a once in a lifetime opportunity for me to experience the power of the Mahamantra.

27. Encounter In Connaught Place

It was a pleasant November afternoon in Delhi. After several busy days I had some time off.

So, I took a stroll around Connaught Place, a stone's throw away from my hotel.

From the corner of my eye, I saw a woman eyeing me. Wait, what was that?

An imperceptible flutter of her eyelids. Yes, definitely a come-hither look!

I turned to face her.

Attractive, in her forties, lounging around, leaning on the walkway's pillar. Wearing a light pink kameez with white salwar.

Sindoor[34] proclaimed marriage.

She smiled at me, a clear invitation.

I could tell that she was a professional, a sex worker.

Deep compassion and curiosity welled up in me.

Who was she and why was she doing what she's doing?

---

[34] *Vermillion powder applied to the parting of hair to indicate marital status of women in India*

I walked up to her.

The smile was warm and welcoming.

"Would you like to join me for coffee?" I asked.

"Yes."

We walked in silence to a coffee shop nearby. I waited until she sat down.

And parked myself across the table. We ordered coffee and sandwiches.

"I'm sorry. I'm not a customer, but I'd like to talk with you if you don't mind."

"That's ok, I don't mind at all."

She began to look at me in a new light, but exactly what I couldn't tell. The waiter arrived with coffee pot, cups, and sandwiches.

I poured her a cup and passed the sandwiches. "Tell me about yourself."

She began to tell her story. Married at 19. 2 kids by 22.

Husband working in a small shop.

Then, an almost fatal accident that left him immobile. Unable to work and earn an income.

Kids got sick, food was scarce, husband's medicines cost a fortune and no income.

No way to repay loans. Trouble from money lenders.

Harassment from men, all of whom assumed she was available. Humiliated, hurt, and beaten for refusing advances.

Running from pillar to post with no family support and no skills whatsoever.

Hungry babies to feed. Husband's pain aggravating daily. Loneliness, despair, destitution.

Until one day something inside broke. Societal hypocrisy can be the route to survival.

A sympathetic acquaintance introduces her to the right circle. And then, slowly, reluctantly it begins.

Income begins to flow with shame and guilt as handmaidens. Danger at every turn.

Safety: physical, emotional, psychological, all at a discount every moment.

Stress and the risk of infection take a toll.

Personal needs be damned, the family can at least eat two square meals.

"I'm so very sorry that you have to suffer all this."

"No need to be sorry, Sir. Actually, you're the first person to listen to my story. No one has ever bothered to even look twice at me. All they see is a sex machine. I'm just a piece of flesh to satisfy their needs. And once they're done, well, I'm thrown out. No one sees or cares about my suffering or my needs. They don't even treat me as a human being. And look at you. You've brought me to this nice coffee shop. Thank you for the izzat, respect, with which you have treated me. I'll never forget you."

I was amazed and deeply impressed with her honesty and dignity. Told her about a few things she could do to learn new skills.

Thanked her and took leave.

She taught me many, many things over coffee that afternoon. That every story has at least 2 sides.

That appearances never tell the full story and assumptions are dangerous. That listening with understanding and care are empowering.

And over and above everything else, every human being deserves respect and acceptance.

28. Nagpur Days

Childhood memories are dominated by playtime and food! And so, Nagpur has always stayed fresh in my memory.

Amma's cooking was delightfully wrapped in mother's love.

Dosas, idlis, omelettes, sandwiches, sambar, dal, roti, you name it and it was all there.

In copious quantities.

Served with the world's best coffee!

The taste and tenderness still linger as fragrances from the past eternal. Life was full of fun and frolic.

The gang was always outside, playing street cricket with tennis balls.

Once, I was batting and thought the ball had missed the chalk marking stumps.

The bowler disagreed. "You're clean bowled."

"No, I'm not. The ball missed the stumps." The argument escalated.

Pushing and shoving.

And finally, the bowler gave me a resounding slap.

My left cheek smarted more with humiliation than hurt.

The previous night Achan had read out from the book he was writing. Christucharitam Life of Christ for children.

The example of Jesus wafted into my consciousness, in the heat of the fight on the street.

"Oh, you've slapped me. That was wrong. But I won't hit you back. Here's my other cheek, you may slap my right cheek too."

I was filled with a sense of pride that I'd remembered Achan's story. The pride was short-lived.

Punctured by a sharp pain.

The bowler had slapped me, hard, again. This time on my right cheek. So much for turning the other cheek.

Now both my cheeks burned.

I learnt painfully when not to turn the other cheek!

As a child, KP Menon Uncle's home was the go-to place for me.

He was Achan's best friend and naturally, his son Shivkumar was mine too.

Shivkumar and me and his younger brother Raju..spent countless hours together playing marbles, gilli-danda[35], pittu[36] et al.

Uncle owned a Jeep-like vehicle which was famous throughout Nagpur. It was named Ottakannan, the One-Eyed Creature.

Because only one of the headlights would work irrespective of any repair!

---

[35] A unique stick and bail game played in India
[36] Tiles and ball..where you had to throw the ball to break a stack of tiles.

I don't know how, but Shivkumar and I were conned into joining a Bharatnatyam class!

There we were, tatta tai ti tai, arms & legs flailing like windmills.

After one class we discovered, mercifully, that Bharatanatyam was not for clowns.

Diwali in Nagpur was joyful, celebrated with all the friends. But one particular Diwali was extremely painful.

Achan was lighting an Anar, a cracker that lit up in a fountain of sparks.

It was not supposed to explode, but it did, in Achan's right hand, his writing hand.

All the skin on his right palm peeled off. Leaving red blisters.

Achan was the picture of calm.

He reassured everyone that he was fine. And then quietly got into the car.

I clambered into the passenger seat next to him.

I was about 9 years old at the time and too shocked for words. He started the car and drove slowly to the hospital.

I still don't quite know how he shifted gears, held the steering wheel and did everything else with his left hand.

Because by now his right hand was a bloody mess.

At the hospital he made me wait in the corridor while the doctor attended to him.

When he came out about 45 minutes later his right hand was swathed in bandages.

For years after this accident Achan couldn't move the fingers of his right hand properly.

Not once did he complain or even wince.

How he produced a prodigious quantity of writing with that painful right hand is beyond me.

Achan's old faithful was a Morris Minor car. A car with a mind of its own.

Once, when he was driving us to school, we saw a car tyre racing away ahead of us.

All of us sneered at the tyre and its separation from Mother Car until the left side of the Morris tilted to the left.

For reasons unknown, leftie had left our Morris. And sped away to seek its fortune independently! I ran after the wayward tyre.

Vaulting over walls and ditches, it came to rest against a recalcitrant wall. Only then could I retrieve it.

Achan guffawed at the sheer ridiculousness of the entire situations! Every night he would read aloud from his daily writing.

Those stories symbolise the love in our sweet home.

A home that was an oasis of encouragement and safety in a dog-eat-dog world.

The tale of "Morris and The Runaway Tyre" has remained a family favourite.

29. Parents

Parents don't often receive the veneration they deserve.

Children grow into adulthood and then soar into the sky of their life.

In the mad rush of living in the fast lane, they, and us in our prime, lose sight of the fundamentals.

How did a helpless baby grow into me?

Who fed me, clothed me, cared for me lovingly so that I could grow?

Under whose watch and watchful eyes and protective umbrella did I become me?

The answer is quite simply: Parents! Amma, Achan!

Both of them spoke with gratitude, reverence and devotion about their parents, every day that I can remember.

Achan lost his parents rather early.

His mother had died and on the 41st day thereafter, his father too passed away of a broken heart.

Achan's pain can hardly be imagined.

Out of that pain came a great composition that has since been set to Raga Sahana in Carnatic music.

It's been performed by the genius, Chitraveena Ravikiran, no less. The song is entitled Mathapitakkale.

Here it is:

MATAPITAKKALE

By V.Madhavan Nair "Mali" Krithi in Shahana Ragam

Adi Talam 2 Kalai Chowkkam

Pallavi

Maathaapithaakkale[37] kai thozhaam ningale[38]

Anupallavi

Kaamitham   ellaam   ekum[39]   kalpaka   tharukkale[40]
Seemayillaatha kripaasaagarangale[41]

Charanam

Thyaagathin moorthikale[42] vaalsalya nidhikale[43]

Snehathin   roopangale[44]   kaatharulkengale[45]   Kanmasha
haarikale[46]   sreemandirangale[47]   Janmadaathaakkale[48]
bhoodevathakale[49]

---

[37] *Mother and Father*
[38] *I fold my hands in reverence to you*
[39] *You, who fulfill all my desires*
[40] *You, the divine, Heavenly Kalpaka trees that provide all that I wish for*
[41] *limitless oceans..of grace and blessings*
[42] *Icons of sacrifice*
[43] *Treasure houses of the purest love*
[44] *Embodiments of love*
[45] *Please protect and bless me*
[46] *Dispellers of darkness and imperfections*
[47] *Temples of auspiciousness and grace*
[48] *Givers of life..to me*
[49] *Gods on Earth*

Mother and Father, I fold my hands in reverence to you. You, who fulfil all my desires

You, the divine, Heavenly Kalpaka[50] trees that provide all that I wish for

Limitless oceans, of grace and blessings

Icons of sacrifice, treasure houses of the purest love

Embodiments of love, please protect and bless us

Dispellers of darkness and imperfections

Temples of auspiciousness and grace

Givers of life to me, Gods on Earth for me

Mother and Father, I fold my hands in reverence to you

Achan once told me, out of great suffering comes great creativity. "Human beings are distilled by suffering to become purer and purer" he would say.

Some of his masterpieces, notably Karnasapatham Kathakali, came out of deep sorrow and stress.

"Matapitakkale" is short and heartfelt.

And it came out of the depths of despair and loss. It ranks undoubtedly amongst his very best works.

---

[50] *Kalpaka Trees (also known as Kalpavriksha, Kalpataru, or Kalpadruma) are mythical wish-fulfilling trees in Indian mythology and Hindu tradition. These trees are considered sacred and are believed to have the power to grant any wish or desire, symbolizing abundance, prosperity, and divine generosity.*
Origin in Mythology: Samudra Manthan (Churning of the Ocean): According to Hindu mythology, the Kalpaka tree emerged during the Samudra Manthan (the churning of the ocean by gods and demons). It was one of the treasures that surfaced from the ocean. It was taken to Indra's paradise (Swarga) and is said to reside there, providing endless bounty

When it is sung or played in Raga Sahana the impact on listeners cannot be described in mere words.

I've yet to see a dry eye when Matapitakkale is rendered or indeed, when some particular padams (broadly, songs) in Karnasapatham are sung.

The common element in all these creations is the stress on the nobler aspects of life: loyalty, devotion, friendship, duty, courage, sacrifice, love.

He would always credit his parents for all his work.

Achan's reverence for his parents was something to experience. And mirrors, exactly, my feelings towards my own parents.

30. Rotary

"You must apply for this scholarship, you'll certainly win it". That was my elder sister Madhavi.

Her belief in me was total. She was a star.

Right through school and college, she stood first in every test and exam.

Our display cases were overflowing with the trophies and prizes she'd won, from debate to sports to music.

She'd even won a prize for Marathi recitation!

Once, when I was about 13 years old, Madhavi, with Amma in tow, marched up to confront my school Principal.

His crime?

He was going to leave me out of a music program for which I'd been selected to play the mridangam.

Madhavi was bristling with indignation and sibling love and loyalty. She and Amma together were a formidable force.

They hauled the Principal over the coals for "discouraging an earnest young boy".

After that, what choice did the hapless Principal have? I played in the program!

So when Madhavi said "Apply," I applied.

If she thought I'd make it, well then, there was no doubt in my mind!

And so, I was awarded the Rotary International Ambassadorial Scholarship for 1981-82 and proceeded to study at Thunderbird.

On my return to India, I was invited to join the Rotary Club of Cochin. Rotarian Suryanarayanan (Suri) was one of my proposers.

Till today, some 40 years later, the joke is that Suri's biggest blunder in life was to propose me to the membership of the club!

I plunged into Rotary with gusto, like fish to water.

The fellowship and camaraderie can only be experienced, not described. The Club made me its President in 1993-94.

In 1991, I was assigned to be the Aide to a senior but out of favour Rotary Past District Governor (PDG) from Vapi, Gujarat.

Rotarian PDG Kalyan Banerji.

Kalyan is a deeply intellectual, brooding Bengali chemical engineer (from Indian Institute of Technology, Kharagpur) who'd made Vapi his Karmabhoomi.

He was fluent not just in Hindi but also Gujarati..and Bengali and English. Brilliant speaker, visionary, inspirational leader.

We got on like a house on fire.

When I saw him off at the airport I said, "Kalyan, I'm sure you're going to be President of Rotary International in a few years."

Kalyan laughed it off.

He was nominated President for 2011-12 only the third Indian in Rotary's century old history to be so anointed.

Right from Day 1 our friendship has been a saga of affection and respect. I was by his side in myriad Rotary and personal challenges.

When the devastating earthquake flattened parts of Gujarat State in India on 26 January 2001, Kalyan and I were in Breach Candy Hospital, Mumbai.

We were with Kalyan's beloved wife Binota who was undergoing dialysis. From the hospital he launched Rotary's relief and rehabilitation efforts.

Such is Kalyan's commitment to service above self through Rotary.

We were able to, amongst other things, launch a website within 100 hours.

The site collected over 2 million USD in donations to Rotary relief projects over a period of time.

When he was nominated President, he was nudged by another President- in-the making to appoint me to the Strategic Planning Committee (SPC) of Rotary International.

When I sat in Rotary International's Board Room in Evanston, IL, USA, as a member of the SPC, I was arguably the only non PDG Rotarian ever to be part of such a high-level committee, a singular honour, thanks to Kalyan's faith in me.

During his visit to Kochi as President Nominee, Kalyan told a hall packed with hundreds of Rotarians,

"You push Madhav and I'll pull him up!"

The message was indirect, but loud and clear.

If I were to be elected District Governor, Kalyan would support my further growth in the international hierarchy of Rotary.

My club, the Rotary Club of Cochin, then got into an emergency meeting and proposed me for Governorship.

I was extremely grateful for this vote of confidence.

For a week I went through the motions but knew this was not for me.

I chose, wisely, I think, to serve Rotary not as Governor, but in other ways.

Over the years, I've provided several Presidents and Directors with concepts and ideas and where necessary, tough feedback.

Since I've had no vested interests, I've always been able to speak my mind freely and focus my attention on the best interests of Rotary.

India has eradicated polio and has, largely, Rotary to thank for it.

The Pulse Polio project saw thousands of Rotarians fan out into the country side.

They administered millions of doses of the polio vaccine to babies for years.

Service Above Self is a guiding principle of Rotary. For me it's a deeply significant spiritual precept.

Isn't it amazing that a temporal organisation is tethered to a spiritual truth? Maybe that explains why Rotary, founded in 1905, is still going strong.

Though it is facing challenges in membership retention in North America, Rotary is growing in power and stature in India.

Perhaps an innate spiritual bent of mind amongst many Indians has something to do with it.

For over 4 decades Rotary has shaped and moulded me.

It has taught me, among other things, how to work with peers. And helped me build lasting friendships. worldwide.

I saw, first hand, how Rotary changes lives.

Most important of all, it has showed me the power of selflessness. And that has changed my life too.

31. Case Of The Unfortunate Barber

Knock, knock.

It was 8 am.

We were in a room at a Urology hospital. Achan had to have a prostate needle biopsy later that morning.

Not a pleasant prospect but Achan was matter of fact about the whole thing.

All of us were just digging into a breakfast, idli-sambar and coffee. Knock, knock, knock.

The knocks changed to a loud banging.

As if I were Usain Bolt and could bolt to the door in 2 seconds flat! Wait! Coming!

The banging reached a crescendo.

Maybe a SWAT team was about to break down the door! I managed to reach the door before it was all over.

Who wants to be shaken so rudely so early in the morning?

I was thoroughly irritated and so were Achan, Amma and Radha. I flung open the door, ready to punch the transgressor.

A slight, older man stood in the veranda.

In his left hand was an uninspiring plastic mug.

In the right he carried rolled newspaper with something in it.

A grumpy look on his face told me that he wasn't happy either.

"I want to shave..."

Before he could complete the sentence, I cut him off. "What? You want to shave?"

"Yes. I have to do it now"

"Now? You want to shave, now?"

"Yes, now."

"In this room?!!"

"Yes. In this room, now."

That's it! I lost my temper.

"Who the hell are you to think you can walk into our room to shave." I was screaming with rage by now.

The gall of the man!

Didn't you get any other room to shave? You had to just had to come here to shave? Couldn't you have shaved at home?

Or gone to a barber?

By now, everyone was thoroughly perplexed. Achan wanted to know if the man was drunk. Amma gnashed her teeth.

Radha wanted to know if he was a hospital employee.

I was barely controlling myself.

The man had already squeezed one foot into the doorway. He was the unrolling the newspaper.

I could see a shaving razor, some shaving soap and a pair of scissors. Now he was in the room!

And making a beeline to the toilet. "What are you doing?

Are you out of your mind?

Coming into a patient's room and demanding to shave!"

He reached the toilet and was about to go inside when I grabbed him by the scruff of his neck.

By now he was terrified. "Sir, sir!"

"What! What?

"You come into our room without permission and have the audacity to go to the toilet to shave?"

I was livid.

But his tone of voice and petrified expression caught my attention. He was trying to say something.

"What are you saying?" I asked.

"Sir, I'm a barber."

"So?"

"I've come to shave…"

"We didn't ask for a shave."

"No, no, Sir."

"What? For God's sake!"

"Sir. Sir, I've come to shave the patient."

It was as though a huge balloon had been pricked.

Achan's guffaw broke the tension.

We burst out laughing.

The poor man was indeed the barber.

And he was here to shave Achan's body prior to the biopsy! He'd been unnerved by my aggression at the door.

And was unable to express himself clearly. I apologised profusely to him.

Everyone was laughing their guts out.

Achan was in total delight at the ridiculousness of the whole thing!

He was so tickled that the doctor didn't feel the need to sedate him too much.

The case of the Unfortunate Barber causes much mirth, even today!

32. Raj Bhavan

On October 16 1905, the Partition of Bengal was officially implemented by Lord Curzon, then Viceroy of India[51].

This was short lived because the Swadeshi Movement ensured that the decision was reversed in 19011[52].

"This is the table at which the Partition of Bengal was finalised".

His Excellency, The Honourable Governor of West Bengal, Dr CV Ananda Bose had invited me to tea in the historic Library of Raj Bhavan, Kolkata.

From his encyclopaedic memory he was giving me the history of the table that we were sitting at!

West Bengal is a crucial border state of India with an external border spanning thousands of kilometres.

When he took oath as Governor of the State of West Bengal it was an important moment in modern Indian history.

---

[51] *The title Viceroy of India was established in 1858 when the British Crown assumed direct control over India from the East India Company. The Viceroy served as the monarch's representative and held supreme authority over British India until independence in 1947, when the role was dissolved and replaced by the Governor-General of independent India - ChatGPT*

[52] *The Swadeshi Movement (1905–1911) was launched in protest against the Partition of Bengal implemented by Lord Curzon. Through widespread boycotts, public demonstrations, and promotion of indigenous goods, the movement galvanized national sentiment. As a result, the British government reversed the partition in 1911 during the Delhi Durbar. - ChatGPT*

Because India is quite literally on the springboard to greatness.

And Dr Ananda Bose is the perfect fit because of his knowledge, erudition and peerless administrative acumen honed for over 40 years in the Indian Administrative Service.

His mastery of language and the business of government is legendary.

Brimming with enthusiasm and positivity, he's been described as a "Man of Ideas" by no less than Prime Minister Narendra Modi himself.

He's been an ardent admirer of Achan and Achan's younger brother, V.P. Nair (a genius in his own right and two term Member of Parliament) for decades.

And dare I say, both of them played an important role in his evolution as a thinker, author and administrator par excellence.

Over the years I've had the good fortune to be associated with him in various areas.

One common element in both our backgrounds is that he too was a Probationary Officer in State Bank of India during the earliest phase of his career.

I was privileged that he had appointed me as Chief, Governor's Advisory Group-Ideation & Operations.

In effect, my role is to share ideas, concepts and ways forward with him, a sounding board of sorts.

Staying at Rajbhavan Kolkata is breathtaking at the very least.

History speaks to you from every pillar, every doorway and indeed, every sofa and chair!

Colonial history, I might add, because it was built in 1803 under the orders of the then Governor General of India, Lord Wellesley[53].

Raj Bhavan was the seat of British power in India for a long time.

It is literally a living museum and a treasure-trove of artefacts and traditions all held within imposing rooms.

For me, though, Raj Bhavan represents something very different. It is the intersection of colonialism and modern India.

At the intersection lies the power and might of the new Indian state.

Raj Bhavan is the concrete manifestation of the rule of law and constitutional propriety inherent in the emergence of a democratic superpower.

So, every time I set foot in Raj Bhavan my heart swells with pride as an Indian.

Because Raj Bhavan is the ultimate symbol of India's hard and soft power.

From the crack CRP commandos equipped with the latest weaponry to the super-competent military Aid De Camp to the Governor, well, the entire environment is one of gravitas and dedication to mighty India.

---

[53] *Lord Wellesley, who served as Governor-General of India from 1798 to 1805, was not referred to as a Viceroy during his tenure. The title "Viceroy" was introduced later, following the Government of India Act of 1858, which transferred control of India from the East India Company to the British Crown. The first official to hold the title of Viceroy was Lord Canning, beginning in 1858. ..ChatGPT o1-mini*

Discussions with HE (His Excellency, The Honourable Governor) are always exciting and stimulating with razor sharp wit and repartee.

Subjects range from Constitutional provisions to economic policy to social imperatives and art and culture.

"Dharma" in particular is an area in which we spend much time. Sometimes we meet at 0600 hrs and at 2130 hrs at other times!

What is common is that once we're in a meeting, there's no telling when we're out!

Tea, refreshments and food are all available at all times with extraordinary hospitality.

Travelling with HE is quite the experience.

It reminds me of the Red Sea parting for Moses!

Traffic is held up; pilot vehicles clear the way and everything is smoother than silk for the convoy.

Security and protocol define every movement, as they should, for such a high constitutional office.

But through it all, HE remains unmoved, approachable, humble and very receptive to ideas.

Its been the privilege of my life to serve in this capacity!

33. Loyalty, Again!

In August 1993, I was at my wit's end.

I had just taken over as President of the Rotary Club of Cochin. It was a blue-blooded club.

With a host of traditions and conventions that went all the way back to 23 August 1937 when it was chartered.

As President, it was up to me to maintain and further the high standards of conduct and competence that had made the Club synonymous with excellence. And that was the challenge I was facing.

Running my company, writing, speaking, travel …all of them took prodigious amounts of time and energy.

I couldn't take the Rotary Club of Cochin lightly.

Being President was not only an honour; it was almost a full-time job! I needed help.

Larene was already my Secretary and doing a wonderful job. But by then she was also handling other responsibilities.

I could tell that she was overloaded.

I desperately needed additional hands to help me organise myself. I needed an additional Secretary.

So, Larene and I set about searching.

One day I was told that a lady was waiting to see me. She was referred by someone as a possible Secretary. I met her immediately.

One look and I knew she was the one. Quiet, slight and dignified.

Calm and centred with an ever-ready smile flashing across her face.

She had quite a bit of experience and I sensed she was quick to learn. Without much ado Mary joined and plunged right in.

Within a short time, she had earned my trust and confidence. If I entrusted her with something I could forget about it.

I was sure that she'd do it perfectly.

In those days I was pretty hot tempered and fiery! Very quickly Mary learnt to deal with my outbursts. She would just smile and get on with it!

No complaints, no moods just a dignified presence that defused all the stress! She took over many things and my work and responsibilities came back into balance.

I was able to discharge my role as the President of the Rotary Club of Cochin smoothly and successfully, thanks to Mary's effectiveness.

Typing, following up, organizing and getting things done were all her forte. In 1993 I had just started to type on the computer myself.

After a while I was pretty fast and was writing directly on the computer. The era of dictation and writing in long hand was well and truly over.

"Hey, Mary, I'm faster than you on the keyboard," was my way of ragging her! Mary was not one of those flashy, showy kinds of people.

She had the kind of inner strength that did not need to be flaunted. And soon I began to realise how sincere she was.

The business was doing reasonably well but cash was certainly hard to come by. I'd bought my first car.

A tenth hand Ambassador that was barely held together by endless tinkering! I'd once driven it to Masinagudi, beyond the Nilgiri mountains.

The return journey was a nightmare!

Breakdown after breakdown ensured that a journey of 8 hours stretched interminably to over 24 hours.

The car was in the workshop more than it was on the road!

And so it was that it was that it was handed over to Sivasakthi Motors for some engine work.

After about five days I was informed that the car was ready. So I went to the workshop to fetch it.

I was in for a shock.

The workshop owner refused to hand over the car unless the bill was paid in cash, then and there.

It was princely sum of Rs 5,000/- and I did not have it on me. Neither did I have it in my bank account.

I had no way of paying the money for at least 3 days.

I tried to reason with the workshop owner but to no avail.

Finally, I called Mary in the office on the landline (cellphones were not yet introduced) and explained the matter.

I asked if she could organise some cash from our corporate account. As usual, Mary was cool as a cucumber.

She said she would call me back at the workshop in half an hour. So I waited, uncomfortable, embarrassed and seething.

Half an hour later, Mary arrived at the workshop, perched precariously on the pillion seat of her brother's motorbike.

She went straight into the workshop owner's office.

Five minutes later she emerged triumphantly with the car keys! We drove off without much incident.

She'd borrowed the money from her brother!

Of course, I made sure that she was paid back immediately.

But she'd sorted out the problem, quickly, without fuss.

She'd saved me from further discomfiture.

That's loyalty for you! Again!

Mary's sure touch continues to make life better for me today, more than three decades later.

She has the confidence and capability to meet anyone, anywhere and get anything done!

I owe her a debt I can never repay!

34. Banking On The Front Lines

Mookandapally Branch, Circa 1981.

On the outskirts of a dusty town named Hosur some 40 km away from Bangalore. My first posting after being confirmed as an Officer, State Bank of India.

Field Officer, in charge of industrial and small-scale sector lending. Age, 25.

Loan portfolio: around Rs 2 crore then, in 1981; worth around Rs 43 crores in 2025[54].

I was this starry-eyed young banker full of idealistic zeal! Brimming with ideas and enthusiasm to contribute to my country. And I was deployed on the front lines of India's economy.

Mookandapally was where the manufacturing revolution was beginning.

Large companies were setting up huge factories; around them an entire ecosystem of ancillaries and small-scale enterprises were sprouting.

---

[54] *Calculated on the basis of an average annual interest rate of 7.22%...ChatGPT 4o as edited by VK Madhav Mohan*

Banking services were critical to the growth of this ecosystem. For a young loan officer, Mookandapally was the place to be! Radha and I had been married for just under a year.

So, Mookandapally was where we were setting up our first home. We arrived at our new house, full of excitement.

The house was small but cosy.

But there was something strange about it. At first, we couldn't figure it out.

And then it hit us.

There were no water pipes or taps in the house!

All of twenty years of age, Radha was perplexed and worried. "What are we going to do about water?" She asked.

A neighbour told us that a "water-man" would bring a barrel of water, in a bullock cart, every alternate day.

This could be used for washing and cleaning; it was better not to ask where water came from!

Drinking water was another story altogether!

I would have to trudge with a bucket for a kilometre every morning to fill it under a common tap.

And so we set up home.

Nothing fancy but a home filled with love and hopes for the future!

Living on the princely salary of around Rs 1500/- per month was a stretch to say the least.

But those were very happy and memorable times! My work was challenging!

I was on the cutting edge of Indian banking.

My boss, the Branch Manager, Subbaram, was a portly officer some 10 years my senior.

He had a penchant for using red pencils to cross out loan proposals.

Once, I had submitted, after much thought, a detailed loan proposal for his approval.

The messenger brought the file back to me after a day or so.

The proposal was practically defaced by a surfeit of red pencil crosses and underlining.

Looking closely, I noticed that Subbaram had nothing to say on the merits or calculations in the proposal.

He had edited my English on a grand scale, with a red pencil, like a teacher scolding an errant pupil!

I saw red!

I stormed into his room and bolted the door from inside. Then, I proceeded to give him a verbal roasting.

The gist of my outburst was that he could keep his English competency to himself or else the heavens would come crashing down on him..and that was putting it politely!

So much for fearing bosses!

Subbaram gave me a wide berth thereafter!

One day a disgruntled partner of one of our borrowers tipped me off about some serious wrongdoing by his partner.

We arranged to meet behind some bushes in Cubbon Park, Bangalore. A true cloak and dagger tryst!

I rode the Bank's scooter into Bangalore.

The man was clearly nervous and afraid because he was snitching on his partner.

He spoke in hushed tones about how the Bank's money was being siphoned off into another bank.

I felt like I was Bond 007!

Armed with this information, I went into the other bank in Bangalore, identified myself as an Officer from State Bank of India and confirmed that my information was indeed accurate.

Not one to shy away from decisive action, I turned up at the borrower's factory next morning.

I had brought along the Bank's huge padlock and seal.

Right under the noses of surly workers carrying steel rods I locked the premises, affixed the bank's seal and initiated legal proceedings to recover the money.

There were at least 50 of them; I was alone and unarmed. Anything could have happened that morning.

Talk about youthful chutzpah!

One afternoon I was busy reviewing the loan accounts under my charge. I heard a commotion from just outside the Bank.

Instinctively I knew there was trouble.

Rushing out I spotted one of the Bank's borrowers.

He was being roundly thrashed by a bunch of provision shop owners from Hosur market.

Interjecting myself between the mob and the borrower I found that he'd been remiss in paying for the provisions that he'd bought.

I rescued him and took him into the Bank.

He told me a story that has left a deep skepticism within me for large companies.

He was a contractor who was running the food canteen for a large automobile factory.

The factory had asked him to provide more food to the workers than had been written in the contract.

The Administration Manager of the factory had verbally assured him that the company would pay him for the additional food.

But of course, they didn't. So he couldn't pay for the additional provisions. The borrower was left deep in debt to the provision suppliers.

Hence the thrashing.

So much for large companies encouraging the growth of smaller businesses! Mookandapally Branch helped me cut my teeth as a leader.

One of the clerks who worked with me, Balu, was a smart aleck. He was about my age; while he was a clerk, I was an Officer.

So he carried a chip on his shoulder.

He was not lodging cheques and presenting them for clearing in a timely manner.

This was creating problems for the borrowers because their accounts were not being credited in time.

The first time I noticed this I went over to Balu and explained gently about the need to make sure that cheques were lodged quickly and sent for clearing so that the amounts could be credited.

I took great pains to show him why all this mattered so much to borrowers. Balu assured me that he would smarten up.

Then it happened again a couple of days later. cheques had piled up. I went over again and asked Balu what had happened.

He gave me a cock and bull story but said he would act immediately. A few days later the situation repeated.

I was firm this time and Balu gave me the same fake assurance. He was testing me!

"This young Officer believes he's so superior to me. Let's see what he's made of." I could almost hear him think.

Balu was also a leader of the Staff Union so he was confident about his own support base and safety.

I had decided on my next course of action and so I waited for the next occasion.

Sure enough, after a few days, I found a pile of unlogged cheques in a desk drawer.

I calmly went over to Balu.

Though I was cool internally, my demeanour and tone of voice was anything but!

I grabbed him by the scruff of his neck and screamed at the top of my voice so everyone in the banking hall could hear!

Essentially what I said was that the worst would befall him if he continued to torture the borrowers with his little powerplay antics.

Balu became an ideal employee thereafter. I had passed my first leadership test!

Mookandapally Branch was the test bed for my professional evolution.

Hosur in those days was a village that had stumbled into becoming a small town. It boasted of a lone movie theatre, torn seats, filthy toilets and all!

Saturday evenings would find us in the balcony watching some movie in Kannada.

During one such evening Radha felt something brush past her feet. She let out a loud gasp and lifted her legs on to the seat.

It was a stray dog!

Many dogs would wander into the balcony class of the theatre. They offered better entertainment than the gyrations on the screen. Perhaps the movies appealed more to the dogs!

Mookandappally and Hosur are deeply etched in our memories as the starting point of our life journey.

35. Quarantine In Belgrade

Covid had extracted a horrendous toll in 2020. The second wave had hit India in April-May 2021.

By July-August international travel had resumed, hesitantly. That's when we had to travel to the US.

Sumitra, our daughter, was expecting her baby in end September, 2021. Wow! I couldn't believe that I was going to be a granddad soon!

Travel was iffy at best.

Quarantine restrictions were in full force. Flight options were few and expensive. Routes were outlandish!

We researched every option as thoroughly as possible. From India to Doha to New York.

From India to Mexico to New York. From India to Egypt to New York.

There was no question of flying direct to the US.

Every option mandated a 15-day quarantine in a third country just before landing in the US.

Finally, we zeroed in on Kochi-Dubai-Belgrade.

We'd do the quarantine in Belgrade, Serbia for 15 days.

Then we'd fly Belgrade-Warsaw-New York.

Amidst great uncertainty, risk and opaque documentation we boarded for Dubai on 18th of August 2021.

We were literally flying into the unknown.

Kochi to Dubai and then after a 2-hour layover, onward to Belgrade. Both of us, Radha and me, looked and felt like aliens!

Kitted out in face shields, face masks and gloves. Uncomfortable and apprehensive.

We landed in Belgrade, Serbia in the evening, local time.

Our chauffeur was a young, rude Serb who made it a point to tell us that waiting was not his job.

Waiting was what he had to do because on-arrival RT PCR tests were mandatory before we could get out of the airport.

It took us a full 90 minutes before we could leave the terminal. The chauffeur was grumpy.

He was making all kinds of sarcastic comments about Indian travellers.

Belgrade was swamped by scared, desperate Indians who had to travel onward to many destinations.

It had become a popular pitstop for quarantine! Quarantine tourism!

The driver's comments became a little too much.

Time to act decisively!

I grabbed him by the arm and told him sternly to shut up. My aggression took him by surprise.

Least expected from a scared, docile Indian! The man's demeanour changed immediately. He became subdued to the point of servility.

He took our luggage, loaded it all into the car and off we went to the hotel.

Yet another lesson in dealing with a bully, albeit fraught with high risk in a strange country in COVID times!

Driving through Belgrade reminded me of the old Soviet bloc.

Even though Marshal Tito's Non-Aligned Yugoslavia was supposedly independent I could spot the vestiges of Soviet influence.

Gray, forbidding apartment and office blocks lining wide boulevards. The city was of course trying very hard to don a European look.

Steel and glass, flowers and street music were jostling with cobbled streets and massive official looking buildings.

A rather quaint mixture of old-world charm, cold war tensions, burgeoning modernity and free spirit!

Flavours and shades of Europe, but at half the cost!

The quarantine rules in Serbia were strict even though the population cared two hoots for vaccination!

We were not allowed to step outside our room for the first 7 days and nights.

Vegetarian food choices were minimal since Serbia is a full-on meat-eating country.

So for more than a week we were eating bread, pasta in pesto sauce and undercooked rice with a smattering of vegetables and turmeric.

Three times a day there would be knock on the door at meal times. Opening the door, we would find our food placed on the floor outside. Like prisoners being fed a subsistence diet.

I could well imagine being locked in solitary confinement.

Except that this was a hotel and we were guests paying through our noses for the privilege of being prisoners.

After 7 days and many RT PCR tests later, we were let out of the room; we could now move around the hotel and go to the restaurant for meals.

We were only allowed to move out of the hotel after 12 days. Quarantine confinement was uniquely charming!

Life was simple. We lived from spare meal to spare meal. No meetings, emails or work.

Workouts, meditation, movies, news, music. The sound of silence was all pervading.

Peace manifested within!

What a change from the routine!

We explored Belgrade, a city of some 1.3 million free spirted people full of buildings with Slavic and Ottoman architecture jostling with the uninspiring grey blocks of former Yugoslavia.

We found a restaurant named St. Mark's Place located on the Bulevar Kralja Aleksandra 17, serving fluffy omelettes, soft breads, mixed cereals and muffins for breakfast, a 20-minute walk from our hotel.

We recruited Alex, a smart chauffeur to driver us around the city.

He took us to the Temple of Saint Sava, built in the Byzantine style and filled with beautiful paintings, murals and chandeliers.

It is an enchanting spiritual sanctuary set amidst a very turbulent past.

After nourishment for the soul, we crossed the street to Pizza Bar where we gorged on delightful food for the body!

We wandered around Skarlina Street and Michaelova Street, window shopping and savouring the fresh air and sound of music.

From the Belgrade Fortress we looked down at the confluence of two rivers. The Danube and Sava came together gently like two bodies uniting in one soul.

The top of the Gardio Tower gave us a panoramic view of the Danube and city of Belgrade, sea of tiles and roof tops each telling of the story of war and peace over the centuries underneath them.

We drove past Zemun, a city that was annexed by Serbia some 200 years ago after much bloodletting.

Walking along quay of the River Danube we saw row boats navigating gingerly past clumsy ducks and graceful swans, each secure in its own place.

The highlight of our free but forced stay in Belgrade was a two-hour drive to Novi Sad where we met the revered spiritual Guru, Mohanji at the Petrovaradian Fortress, a beautiful fort overlooking the city.

Mohanji was the epitome of love. He welcomed us with all his heart and spent over two hours in the open-air restaurant at the fort in Novi Sad.

We could experience the depth of his spirituality and the expanse of his influence and following.

We basked in the presence and blessings of an enlightened being!

One day we were walking down a street and came upon a small pizza place. Peering in we could see a lone middle-aged matron pottering around.

We stepped in and instantly were overwhelmed with the smell of fresh, homemade cheese and bread.

The pizza, made in a small wood fire oven, was just about the best we've ever had!

We could actually taste the sincerity, love and hard work of that lone woman who had poured her all into her work.

We were scheduled to fly out of Belgrade to New York via Warsaw on 3rd of September 2021.

Travel was severely disrupted and COVID rules were changing in real-time in those days.

A sixth sense led me to the airport on 2 September 2021, a full 24 hours ahead of our travel; I just wanted to check on the validity of our tickets and documentation.

Sure enough, we were told that Lot Airlines could not fly us to Warsaw to connect to the Warsaw-New York flight.

Much discussion and high stress ensued.

Visions of being stranded in this far away country floated in front of my eyes. I used all my powers of persuasion.

Natalya of Lot Airlines, Belgrade Airport, spoke at length on our behalf to the Immigration Authorities in Warsaw Airport.

All to no avail!

The rules had changed!

We simply couldn't travel the next day to the US from Belgrade! So we had to do some fancy footwork.

The only feasible option was to fly back to Doha and then connect to New York from there.

I leaned on our travel agent to get us tickets on this route in record time.

Finally, we left Belgrade on the 3rd of September 2021 to New York, as per schedule but via a totally different route.

A two steps forward and one step back kind of a journey! Quarantine in Belgrade was enjoyable.

I learnt that we actually need very little to be happy.

All this to-ing and fro-ing with unremitting busy-ness is very overrated! Simplicity and inner peace are all that matter and available to us for the taking.

Many times, my mind wanders back into the peaceful sanctum of that quiet place in Belgrade.

Memories of the hotel room seasoned with the taste of pasta with pesto still linger!

Maybe I should get back into quarantine!

V.K.Madhav Mohan

About the Author

V.K. Madhav Mohan is a renowned Corporate Mentor whose transformative thought leadership has reshaped businesses across India, Sri Lanka, Qatar, and the USA. As a trusted mentor to CEOs and executives, he has guided organizations through periods of remarkable growth, including guiding an agro-chemical company from $60 million to $6.5 billion in global sales while increasing revenues and cash surpluses multiple times for research and healthcare institutions.

Madhav Mohan's distinguished career includes serving as the youngest director at one of India's largest banks and as Chief Advisor to the Governor of West Bengal. His expertise extends to higher education, where he serves on the boards of several leading universities across India, including Calcutta University.

A prolific author, and an influential voice on LinkedIn, his published works include "Lonely at the Top: Reflections of a Mentor" , "Three Word Truths - Aphorisms For Life", English Translation of "MaliBhagavatam: Divine Stories of SriKrishna for Children" and over 700 original writings on leadership, man agement, economics, and personal development. His popular Military Lead ership Series on YouTube translates military principles into corporate deci sion-making practices.

Though a Global citizen who has delivered more than 5,000 lectures world wide, Madhav Mohan lives in Kochi, Kerala, India from where he continues to mentor leaders and shape organizational futures all over the world, in person and online, through his signature Corporate Mentorship & Personal Growth programs, lectures and writings.

www.ingramcontent.com/pod-product-compliance
Lightning Source LLC
Chambersburg PA
CBHW031129130726
47988CB00006B/2288

ESSAI

SUR

L'ÉDUCATION.

J'ai adopté, en me consacrant à l'Éducation de l'Enfance, un mode d'enseignement propre à faciliter l'intelligence des jeunes personnes confiées à mes soins, et à développer leurs moyens. Si ce faible Essai peut être utile à la Jeunesse, si les personnes vouées à l'Instruction l'approuvent, et ne dédaignent pas d'en faire usage, mon but sera rempli.

La plupart des personnes qui dirigent les Maisons destinées à l'Éducation des jeunes Filles s'écartent du vrai but qu'elles se proposaient sans doute d'atteindre, en sacrifiant tout aux apparences, au brillant qui séduit au premier abord, mais qui n'en est pas moins préjudiciable à une

Éducation solide, basée sur cette simplicité qui accompagne presque toujours le vrai mérite. Si elles étaient bien pénétrées des devoirs attachés à cette honorable mais pénible profession, beaucoup seraient d'avance épouvantées des obligations qu'elles s'imposent. Dépositaires de l'autorité maternelle, arbitres du sort de beaucoup de jeunes personnes qui, au sortir de leurs Maisons, rendues à la société pour en faire l'ornement, y portent trop souvent le germe des défauts qu'une Éducation toute superficielle n'a pu corriger ni même modifier. Elles deviennent responsables, pour ainsi dire, des funestes résultats qui en sont ordinairement la suite. Il faut être mère ou l'avoir été pour bien sentir toute l'importance des fonctions respectables d'Institutrice, et pour donner aux Enfans qui nous sont confiés les soins que nous voudrions qui fussent donnés aux nôtres; alors ne résulterait pas cette insouciance coupable et cette sécheresse de cœur qui portent trop souvent à user de violence envers des êtres intéressans qui, par leur seule faiblesse, réclament notre indulgence et notre appui.

Il est pour ainsi dire de l'essence de beaucoup d'Institutions d'inspirer aux jeunes Personnes un fol amour-propre, qui porte en elles,
jusqu'à l'excès, le désir de plaire, le goût des
vaines parures, une aversion décidée pour tout
ce qui gêne l'esprit et l'assujettit à des règles.
La coquetterie, que l'on s'étudie à leur inspirer
dès l'âge le plus tendre, ne sert qu'à dégrader
leur âme, et à préparer tous les maux qui les
affligent dans le cours de leur vie, plutôt que
d'orner leur esprit de connaissances utiles et
solides, et verser, dans l'âme de ces jeunes
Élèves, les semences de toutes les vertus. L'É-
ducation de ces jeunes Filles passe pour être
finie dès qu'on a réussi à leur donner de futiles
talens, qui servent à flatter l'amour-propre des
parens. On attache auprès de ces Enfans des
maîtres rarement éclairés, chez qui tout le
talent se trouve concentré dans une misérable
routine, dont leur génie borné ne leur permet
pas de s'écarter, même lorsque les circonstances
le demandent. L'aspérité du ton de ces person-
nages, la gravité de leur maintien, les pénitences
dont ils ont grand soin d'être prodigues, tout
en eux ne peut pas manquer d'inspirer cette

basse terreur qui doit conduire à la plus abjecte humiliation.

Combien il importe cependant que les jeunes Personnes destinées à figurer dans la société aient l'esprit éclairé et orné, le raisonnement sûr, les mœurs pures; qu'elles chérissent la vertu par principes; qu'elles sachent enfin puiser dans les meilleures sources la règle de leur conduite et de leur vie. Mais quelle Éducation leur donne-t-on dans la plupart des Pensions? Quelles leçons reçoivent-elles sur le respect et l'amour qu'elles doivent avoir pour la religion sainte dans laquelle elles sont nées? Par quels exercices de l'esprit leur donne-t-on les connaissances qui doivent orner ou éclairer leur âme? Des personnes souvent remplies de fausses maximes pourront-elles apprendre à de semblables êtres à élever leurs enfans? et cependant, a dit Platon, ce sont les mères qui peuvent les premières se faire entendre de leurs enfans; si en effet, dès les premiers momens de l'enfance, les mères se trouvaient capables d'entretenir leurs enfans de tout ce qui a rapport à la vertu, au courage, aux bonnes mœurs; de tout ce qui peut inspirer et faire goûter l'amour de l'étude, des sciences et des beaux arts. Ne serait-il pas naturel d'attendre de ces premières impressions les plus heureux effets; surtout lorsque la raison, éclairée et affermie par les secours de l'Éducation, achève-rait de démontrer à ces enfans la vérité et l'uti-lité des premiers principes qu'ils auraient reçus, lorsque leur jugement développé les rendrait capables de discerner eux-mêmes le beau, l'hon-nête et l'utile, et d'être sensibles à la honte et au mépris attachés à tout ce qui est honteux ou vicieux.

Si les mères de la génération présente veulent affranchir un jour leurs filles du joug auquel les asservit leur ignorance, qu'elles les confient à des personnes éclairées qui puissent choisir elles-mêmes les meilleures méthodes pour réussir dans l'Éducation de la jeunesse; elles appren-dront chez les Spartiates à rendre leurs Élèves sobres, tempérans, vertueux, courageux; chez les Athéniens à les rendre sages, studieux, éclairés; chez les Romains à les former aux plus héroïques vertus; chez les Germains elles puise-ront les grands modèles d'humanité, de bienfai-sance et de grandeur d'âme. Enfin, dans toutes ces fécondes écoles, elles apprendront à leurs

Élèves à chérir et respecter leurs parens, à se
complaire dans leurs enfans, à n'avoir pas de
plus intéressante occupation que celle de leur
inspirer l'amour du beau, de l'honnête, d'é-
clairer leur intelligence, d'orner leur esprit, de
chercher à découvrir leurs talens, et de les
cultiver lorsqu'ils seront reconnus.

Qu'on ne soit pas assez injuste pour me prê-
ter, dans ces réflexions, le dessein de nuire aux
personnes qui tiennent leur existence de cette
profession, ni le projet insensé d'étendre, sur
toutes les classes en général, ce nouveau plan
d'Éducation; je sais combien il serait absurde
et nuisible de prétendre soustraire à leur desti-
nation différentes classes; c'est donc aux mères,
dont les enfans doivent figurer un jour dans la
société, que je m'adresse : le seul bien qui
pourra résulter de l'exécution de mes idées pour
les autres, sera sans doute celui de l'imitation;
elles s'empresseront, d'après la même impulsion
qui les régit aujourd'hui, de copier les heureux
modèles qu'elles auront devant les yeux, et n'y
trouvant plus que des principes de religion et
de vertu, il est aisé de penser qu'elles se déta-
cheront bientôt de cette espèce de luxe, de

cette coquetterie, de cet esprit d'irréligion, de ce dégoût de leur état qu'elles ont malheureusement puisé dans nos mœurs actuelles.

Ce projet n'est pas d'une exécution impossible; les femmes capables d'y être employées sont sans doute en petit nombre; mais il en est cependant qui se sont élevées au-dessus des préjugés, qui ont osé s'adonner aux sciences et aux arts. C'est donc aux Chefs d'Institutions à en faire la distinction. C'est surtout parmi les êtres qu'une chaîne de malheurs condamne à l'oubli, que seront trouvés les sujets vraiment estimables.

DE LA MANIÈRE D'ENSEIGNER.

On ne saurait bien enseigner ce que l'on sait mal; mais on peut enseigner mal ce que l'on sait bien. Le talent de bien montrer n'est pas toujours joint au savoir. Ce talent s'acquiert et se perfectionne, comme tous les autres, par l'exercice. Il faut étudier le caractère de chacun des enfans qui nous sont confiés, servir leur faible, flatter leur amour-propre, intéresser leur cœur, exciter leur curiosité en leur laissant toujours désirer pour le lendemain ce que vous auriez pu leur apprendre de suite ; ne point les fatiguer par des études forcées. Il faut avoir grand soin d'apprendre à ceux qu'on instruit la manière de bien étudier ; il ne faut rien négliger pour leur inspirer le goût de l'étude et du travail, sans lequel il n'est pas possible de faire de grands progrès. Il faut être bon logicien pour posséder parfaitement l'art d'enseigner les préceptes et les règles que donne la logique, perfectionnant la manière de raisonner et de mettre dans le plus grand jour tout ce qu'on dit et qu'on écrit.

Le but des bons Maîtres doit être de cultiver l'esprit de leurs Élèves, pour régler leur cœur et les rendre plus sages et plus hommes de bien. Ceux qui sont chargés d'enseigner à la Jeunesse doivent avoir grand soin de l'accoutumer à n'estimer et n'admirer que le vrai mérite, sous la livrée même de la misère ; à préférer les actions de bonté et de générosité à toutes celles qui attirent le plus les yeux et l'admiration des hommes ; ils doivent, si ce sont des Filles, travailler principalement à les rendre bonnes filles, bonnes mères et bonnes épouses. Les maîtres doivent tâcher de se faire aimer de leurs

Élèves, afin de leur faire mieux goûter ce qu'ils leur enseignent. S'ils les rebutent par leurs manières, ils leur donnent de l'éloignement pour ce qu'ils veulent leur apprendre : l'estime qu'on fait d'une chose produit l'envie d'y parvenir, et abrège le chemin qui y conduit; on ne néglige rien, et rien ne coûte pour y arriver. Il faut donc faire aimer ce qu'on enseigne, et s'appliquer à en faire bien sentir tout le prix.

Rien n'est plus utile que de faire souvent des questions à ceux qu'on instruit, les exciter à en faire, et répondre avec plaisir quand ils les font.

Le meilleur moyen de les bien instruire et de leur former l'esprit, c'est de leur faire trouver ce qu'on veut leur apprendre. Pour cet effet, il est nécessaire de leur fournir des principes d'où ils puissent tirer des conséquences qui leur découvrent ce dont il s'agit : on est charmé de pouvoir s'attribuer quelque part dans les découvertes qu'on doit aux lumières des autres.

On doit éviter d'entasser preuves sur preuves, quand il ne s'agit pas de prouver un fait par les circonstances. Si les preuves sont démonstra-tives, une suffit pour convaincre; si elles ne le sont pas, la multitude ne sert guère qu'à montrer l'impuissance où l'on est de démontrer ce qu'on veut prouver; un grand nombre de preuves charge la mémoire et fatigue plus ordinairement qu'il n'éclaire.

Pour rendre attentifs ceux à qui on parle, il est nécessaire de mettre les choses dans leur vrai point de vue, et de les proposer sous différens jours, la variété qui plaît, soit dans ce qu'on dit, soit dans la manière de le dire, tient en haleine ceux qui écoutent. Il faut savoir faire naître, dans l'esprit de ses auditeurs, des idées toujours nouvelles et si bien arrangées, qu'elles lui présentent toujours quelque chose de plus frappant.

On ne doit proposer de difficultés que pour faire briller la vérité; en les réfutant, on ne doit avoir d'autre vue que de la débarrasser des nuages de l'erreur et du mensonge. Quiconque enseigne, doit enseigner des choses claires, qu'on conçoive aisément; des choses distinctes, qu'on comprenne sans embarras; des choses utiles, qui soutiennent l'attention; des choses rangées de façon que les unes suivent les autres, et qu'on puisse les retenir facilement. Il est inutile de prendre bien des précautions pour instruire, si on n'a pas soin de montrer en même temps la manière de retenir ce qu'on enseigne.

Une chose bien digne de l'attention de ceux qui sont chargés d'instruire, c'est de prévenir ou de détruire l'irrégulière liaison d'idées dans l'esprit de ceux qu'ils instruisent.

La Logique, en perfectionnant l'esprit, perfectionne aussi le cœur, puisqu'en nous faisant penser juste, elle nous fait pratiquer la vertu.

Pour faire aimer l'étude aux enfans, il ne faut pas les en accabler; au contraire, il faut la leur faire désirer en la leur rendant agréable et variée. S'ils ont témoigné quelque déplaisir à s'y livrer, il faut les en priver entièrement et tout-à-coup, sans pour cela les laisser se livrer à la dissipation et aux jeux. Vous les verrez bientôt, ennuyés de rester inactifs tandis que d'autres s'occupent, vous redemander cette étude avec prière et comme une faveur. Leur zèle n'en sera alors que plus ardent par la privation qu'ils auront éprouvée.

Quant à la Religion, base de l'Éducation, il faut leur en faire aimer les principes avant de leur en faire pratiquer les préceptes, leur inspirer l'amour du bien dans la seule vue de plaire à Dieu, et non les effrayer des peines de l'enfer ; la crainte produit moins de bonnes actions que la reconnaissance. Appliquez-vous donc à leur inspirer ce dernier sentiment, et ils rempliront avec zèle, et pour ainsi dire d'eux-mêmes, leurs devoirs envers Dieu et envers les hommes, et sur toute chose qu'ils apprennent de bonne heure à ne pas faire aux autres ce qu'ils ne voudraient pas qui leur fût fait à eux-mêmes. Divin précepte, source de tout bien et de toute justice.

Quelques années d'exercice et d'expérience m'ont prouvé qu'on pouvait instruire et diriger les Enfans sans leur infliger toutes ces ridicules et humiliantes pénitences adoptées par l'usage, et dont aucun Chef d'Institution n'a encore eu l'idée de s'écarter, persuadés sans doute qu'il faut se faire craindre de ses Élèves pour s'en faire obéir ; qu'ils essayent bien plutôt à s'en faire aimer, et ils reviendront de l'erreur grossière qui les régit. Aucun ne s'est-il donc point encore aperçu du dépit que doit nécessairement éprouver une jeune Enfant qui, les deux genoux en terre une heure plus ou moins, attend humblement, aux pieds de ses compagnes, qu'il plaise à ses maîtres de prendre pitié de sa faiblesse, et d'abréger le temps de son humiliante exposition, ou qu'il survienne quelque personne à la considération de laquelle on accorde la grâce du patient. D'autres, par de ridicules mascarades, telle qu'un bonnet d'âne et souquenille surnommée robe de pénitence, espèrent inspirer le goût de l'étude à leurs Élèves, qui cèdent à la force sans se soumettre, et prennent en aversion ceux qui les dirigent.

Qu'elles raisonnent bien plutôt avec leurs Élèves, qu'elles excitent leur amour-propre, le flattant en prodiguant les louanges et les récompenses à celles qui les ont méritées, et qu'elles excitent, par ces moyens doux, dans les autres, le désir de les imiter.

Pour se charger de diriger des Enfans, il faut les aimer par goût, se plaire avec eux, et s'y dévouer entièrement. J'ai assez étudié le caractère de l'Enfance pour être convaincue que, quelques difficiles à diriger que soient certains sujets, la douceur et la patience seules peuvent les amener à se corriger de leurs mauvaises habitudes et à les détester. La rudesse ne saurait vaincre la rudesse ; l'entêtement, chez les enfans, se fortifie par l'opiniâtreté que l'on met trop souvent à user de violence envers eux : si les moyens doux restent sans effet, du moins n'en produisent-ils point de mauvais ; il faut donc, dans ce dernier cas, abandonner plutôt pendant quelque temps, l'enfant à lui-même, ne pas avoir l'air de s'y intéresser en aucune manière ; vous le verrez alors, humilié de l'indifférence qu'on lui témoigne, faire un heureux retour sur lui-même, afin de ramener à lui l'attention de ses maîtres.

Une chose très-importante à éviter dans une Maison d'Éducation, c'est la préférence marquée accordée trop souvent à ceux des Enfans qui en sont redevables au rang ou à la fortune de leurs parens, bien plus qu'à leur propre mérite ; cette injustice est d'autant plus blâmable qu'il doit, pour le bien général, régner dans une classe une parfaite égalité, sans distinction de rang, d'état ni de fortune.

On ne doit pas négliger d'orner la mémoire des enfans de fables, d'historiettes morales et amusantes, qui ne laissent, dans leur petite ima-gination, que des impressions douces, agréables, qui leur apprennent à aimer le bien, sans con-naître les maux qui naissent des passions.

Pour enseigner la Géographie, l'Histoire, il est nécessaire de leur en faire faire des extraits, ce qui grave mieux dans leur mémoire que d'apprendre par cœur, et répéter comme des perroquets, sans comprendre ce qu'ils disent.

Pour leur former le style, rien n'est meilleur que de leur faire écrire des petites lettres, n'importe sur quel sujet et à qui elles sont adressées, pourvu qu'elles ne s'écartent pas de la vraisemblance.

Après la Lecture et l'Écriture, les principes de Grammaire doivent être les premiers donnés aux Enfans; il est bien essentiel de la leur expli-quer, jusqu'à ce qu'ils la comprennent assez pour l'expliquer eux-mêmes. Vous demandez à un Enfant *ce que c'est que la Grammaire;* il répond, d'après le livre qu'il a entre les mains, que c'est *l'art de parler et d'écrire correctement;* il faut d'abord qu'il sache ce que c'est que *l'art,* et ce que signifie le mot *correctement.* C'est par ces explications scrupuleuses sur toutes choses, que vous parviendrez à leur meubler la tête de choses utiles et qu'ils n'oublient jamais, par la raison qu'ils les savent par principes.

D'après l'exposé que j'ai donné ci-dessus de chaque partie essentielle d'une Éducation suivie, je crois n'avoir rien à ajouter pour prouver combien il est important, pour les Mères de Famille, de confier l'Éducation de leurs Filles aux soins de personnes mûries par l'expérience, et capables de les seconder.

FIN.

IMPRIMERIE DE LEBÈGUE, RUE DES NOYERS, N° 8.